# Learn Latin with Beginner Stories - Fabularum Aesopiarum

HypLern Interlinear Project
www.hyplern.com

First edition: 2025, September

Author: Phaedrus
Translation: Camilo Andrés Bonilla Carvajal PhD, Dr Th. van den End
Foreword: Camilo Andrés Bonilla Carvajal PhD

ISBN: 978-1-988830-57-5

kees@hyplern.com
www.hyplern.com

# Learn Latin with Beginner Stories - Fabularum Aesopiarum

*Interlinear Latin to English*

## Author
Phaedrus

## Translation
Camilo Andrés Bonilla Carvajal PhD, Dr Th. van den End

HypLern Interlinear Project
www.hyplern.com

# The HypLern Method

Learning a foreign language should not mean leafing through page after page in a bilingual dictionary until one's fingertips begin to hurt. Quite the contrary, through everyday language use, friendly reading, and direct exposure to the language we can get well on our way towards mastery of the vocabulary and grammar needed to read native texts. In this manner, learners can be successful in the foreign language without too much study of grammar paradigms or rules. Indeed, Seneca expresses in his sixth epistle that "Longum iter est per praecepta, breve et efficax per exempla[1]."

The HypLern series constitutes an effort to provide a highly effective tool for experiential foreign language learning. Those who are genuinely interested in utilizing original literary works to learn a foreign language do not have to use conventional graded texts or adapted versions for novice readers. The former only distort the actual essence of literary works, while the latter are highly reduced in vocabulary and relevant content. This collection aims to bring the lively experience of reading stories as directly told by their very authors to foreign language learners.

Most excited adult language learners will at some point seek their teachers' guidance on the process of learning to read in the foreign language rather than seeking out external opinions. However, both teachers and learners lack a general reading technique or strategy. Oftentimes, students undertake the reading task equipped with nothing more than a bilingual dictionary, a grammar book, and lots of courage. These efforts often end in frustration as the student builds mis-constructed nonsensical sentences after many hours spent on an aimless translation drill.

Consequently, we have decided to develop this series of interlinear translations intended to afford a comprehensive edition of unabridged texts. These texts are presented as they were originally written with no changes in word choice or order. As a result, we have a translated piece conveying the true meaning under every word from the original work. Our readers receive then two books in just one volume: the original version and its translation.

The reading task is no longer a laborious exercise of patiently decoding unclear and seemingly complex paragraphs. What's more, reading becomes an enjoyable and meaningful process of cultural, philosophical and linguistic learning. Independent learners can then acquire expressions and vocabulary while understanding pragmatic and socio-cultural dimensions of the target language by reading in it rather than reading about it.

Our proposal, however, does not claim to be a novelty. Interlinear translation is as old as the Spanish tongue, e.g. "glosses of [Saint] Emilianus", interlinear bibles in Old German, and of course James Hamilton's work in the 1800s. About the latter, we remind the readers, that as a revolutionary freethinker he promoted the publication of Greco-Roman classic works and further pieces in diverse languages. His effort, such as ours, sought to lighten the exhausting task of looking words up in large glossaries as an educational practice: "if there is any thing which fills reflecting men with melancholy and regret, it is the waste of mortal time, parental money, and puerile happiness, in the present method of pursuing Latin and Greek[2]".

Additionally, another influential figure in the same line of thought as Hamilton was John Locke. Locke was also the philosopher and translator of the Fabulae AEsopi in an interlinear plan. In 1600, he was already suggesting that interlinear texts, everyday communication, and use of the target language could be the most appropriate ways to achieve language learning:

> ...the true and genuine Way, and that which I would propose, not only as the easiest and best, wherein a Child might, without pains or Chiding, get a Language which others are wont to be whipt for at School six or seven Years together...[3]

---

1   "The journey is long through precepts, but brief and effective through examples". Seneca, Lucius Annaeus. (1961) Ad Lucilium Epistulae Morales, vol. I. London: W. Heinemann.

2   In: Hamilton, James (1829?) History, principles, practice and results of the Hamiltonian system, with answers to the Edinburgh and Westminster reviews; A lecture delivered at Liverpool; and instructions for the use of the books published on the system. Londres: W. Aylott and Co., 8, Pater Noster Row. p. 29.

3   In: Locke, John. (1693) Some thoughts concerning education. Londres: A. and J. Churchill. pp. 196-7.

# Who can benefit from this edition?

We identify three kinds of readers, namely, those who take this work as a search tool, those who want to learn a language by reading authentic materials, and those attempting to read writers in their original language. The HypLern collection constitutes a very effective instrument for all of them.

1. For the first target audience, this edition represents a search tool to connect their mother tongue with that of the writer's. Therefore, they have the opportunity to read over an original literary work in an enriching and certain manner.
2. For the second group, reading every word or idiomatic expression in its actual context of use will yield a strong association between the form, the collocation, and the context. This will have a direct impact on long term learning of passive vocabulary, gradually building genuine reading ability in the original language. This book is an ideal companion not only to independent learners but also to those who take lessons with a teacher. At the same time, the continuous feeling of achievement produced during the process of reading original authors both stimulates and empowers the learner to study[1].
3. Finally, the third kind of reader will notice the same benefits as the previous ones. The proximity of a word and its translation in our interlinear texts is a step further from other collections, such as the Loeb Classical Library. Although their works might be considered the most famous in this genre, the presentation of texts on opposite pages hinders the immediate link between words and their semantic equivalence in our native tongue (or one we have a strong mastery of).

---

1  Some further ways of using the present work include:

1. As you progress through the stories, focus less on the lower line (the English translation). Instead, try to read through the upper line, staying in the foreign language as long as possible.
2. Even if you find glosses or explanatory footnotes about the mechanics of the language, you should make your own hypotheses on word formation and syntactical functions in a sentence. Feel confident about inferring your own language rules and test them progressively. You can also take notes concerning those idiomatic expressions or special language usage that calls your attention for later study.
3. As soon as you finish each text, check the reading in the original version (with no interlinear or parallel translation). This will fulfil the main goal of this

collection: bridging the gap between readers and original literary works, training them to read directly and independently.

## Why interlinear?

Conventionally speaking, tiresome reading in tricky and exhausting circumstances has been the common definition of learning by texts. This collection offers a friendly reading format where the language is not a stumbling block anymore. Contrastively, our collection presents a language as a vehicle through which readers can attain and understand their authors' written ideas.

While learning to read, most people are urged to use the dictionary and distinguish words from multiple entries. We help readers skip this step by providing the proper translation based on the surrounding context. In so doing, readers have the chance to invest energy and time in understanding the text and learning vocabulary; they read quickly and easily like a skilled horseman cantering through a book.

Thereby we stress the fact that our proposal is not new at all. Others have tried the same before, coming up with evident and substantial outcomes. Certainly, we are not pioneers in designing interlinear texts. Nonetheless, we are nowadays the only, and doubtless, the best, in providing you with interlinear foreign language texts.

## Handling instructions

Using this book is very easy. Each text should be read at least three times in order to explore the whole potential of the method. The first phase is devoted to comparing words in the foreign language to those in the mother tongue. This is to say, the upper line is contrasted to the lower line as the following example shows:

| "Quanta | res | indigno | loco | iaces!" |
|---------|-----|---------|------|---------|
| (You) how (fine) | a thing | in an unworthy | place | you lay lies |

The second phase of reading focuses on capturing the meaning and sense of the original text. As readers gain practice with the method, they should be able to focus on the target language without getting distracted by the translation. New users of the method, however, may find it helpful to cover the translated lines with a piece of paper as illustrated in the image below. Subsequently, they try to understand the meaning of every word, phrase, and entire sentences in the target language itself, drawing on the translation only when necessary. In this phase, the reader should resist the temptation to look at the translation for every word. In doing so, they will find that they are able to understand a good portion of the text by reading directly in the target language, without the crutch of the translation. This is the skill we are looking to train: the ability to read and understand native materials and enjoy them as native speakers do, that being, directly in the original language.

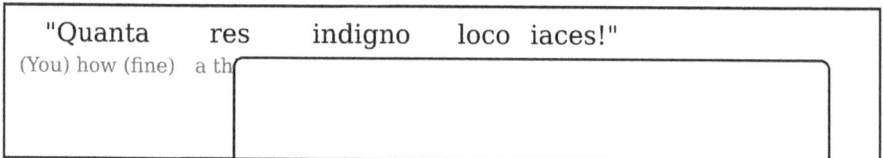

"Quanta     res     indigno    loco  iaces!"
(You) how (fine)   a th

In the final phase, readers will be able to understand the meaning of the text when reading it without additional help. There may be some less common words and phrases which have not cemented themselves yet in the reader's brain, but the majority of the story should not pose any problems. If desired, the reader can use an SRS or some other memorization method to learning these straggling words.

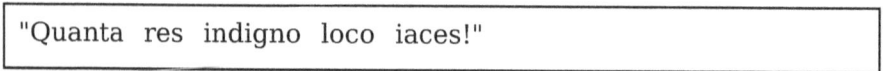

"Quanta  res  indigno  loco  iaces!"

Above all, readers will not have to look every word up in a dictionary to read a text in the foreign language. This otherwise wasted time will be spent concentrating on their principal interest. These new readers will tackle authentic texts while learning their vocabulary and expressions to use in further communicative (written or oral) situations. This book is just one work from an overall series with the same purpose. It really helps those who are afraid of having "poor vocabulary" to feel confident about reading directly in the language. To all of them and to all of you, welcome to the amazing experience of living a foreign language!

## Additional tools

Check out shop.hyplern.com or contact us at info@hyplern.com for free mp3s (if available) and free empty (untranslated) versions of the eBooks that we have on offer.

For some of the older eBooks and paperbacks we have Windows, iOS and Android apps available that, next to the interlinear format, allow for a pop-up format, where hovering over a word or clicking on it gives you its meaning. The apps also have any mp3s, if available, and integrated vocabulary practice.

Visit the site hyplern.com for the same functionality online. This is where we will be working non-stop to make all our material available in multiple formats, including audio where available, and vocabulary practice.

# Table of Contents

# LIBER PRIMUS - PROLOGUS

----

PRIMVS    LIBER    ÆSOPIARVM    FABVLARVM
(THE) FIRST    BOOK    OF-AESOPIAN    FABLES

PHÆDRI    LIBERTI   AVGVSTI
OF-PHAEDRUS   FREEDMAN   (OF) AUGUSTUS

Prologus.    Hanc    materiam,    quam    auctor    Aesopus
Prologue    This    matter    which    the-author    Aesop

repperit,    ego    polivi    versibus    senariis.    Est
has-found    I    have-polished    with-verses    of-six-feet-each    Is

duplex    dos    libelli:    quod    movet    risum
two-fold    the-gift    of-the-little-book    that-it    moves    to-laughter

et    quod    monet    vitam    consilio    prudenti.    Si
and    that-it    gives advice    to-life    with-counsel    prudent    If

autem    quis    voluerit    calumniari    quod
however    anyone    would-like    to-find-fault-with    (the fact) that

arbores    loquantur,    non    tantum    ferae,
trees    speak    (and) not    only    the-beasts

**meminerit**         **iocari**      **nos**    **fictis**
let-he-remember    (that we) amuse (ourselves)    we    with-fictitious

**fabulis.**
fables

# I. Lupus et Agnus

----

## I. Lupus et Agnus
1 The-Wolf and the-Lamb

Ad eundem rivum lupus et agnus venerant,
To the-same river-bank a-wolf and a-lamb had-come

compulsi siti. Superior stabat lupus, longeque
compelled by-thirst Above stood the-wolf and-way

inferior agnus. Tunc improba fauce incitatus
below the-lamb Then with-a-wicked mouth the-aroused
{faux5}

latro intulit causam iurgii; "Cur," inquit,
bandit has brought-up a-cause of-dispute Why he-said

"fecisti aquam bibenti turbulentam mihi?"
have-you-made the-water drinking disturbed for-me
{bibens3} (muddy)

Laniger contra, timens: "Qui possum,
The-fleecy one (replied) in opposition fearful How can-I

quaeso, facere quod quereris, lupe?
I-ask do that which you-have-complain Wolf

Liquor decurrit a te ad meos haustus." Ille
The-liquid runs-down from you to my drinking he
(the wolf)

repulsus viribus veritatis ait: "Ante hos sex
repelled by-the-strength of-the-truth says Before these six
{vis5pl}

menses male dixisti mihi". Agnus respondit:
months ill you-have-spoken to me The-lamb replies

"Equidem eram non natus". "Hercle, tuus pater,"
Indeed I-was not born (yet) By-Hercules your father

ille inquit "male dixit mihi"; atque ita
he said ill he-has-spoken to me and thus
(the wolf)

correptum lacerat iniusta nece.
the-having-been-captured (the-wolf) lacerates with-unfair death
(the captured one)

Haec fabula est scripta propter illos homines qui
This fable is written because-of those men who

opprimunt innocentes fictis causis.
oppress the-innocent with-fictitious causes

5

# II. Ranae Petunt Regem

----

II.　Ranae　Petunt　Regem
2　The-Frogs　Ask-for　a-King

Cum　Athenae　florerent　aequis　legibus,
When　Athens　was-flourishing　with-fair　laws
　　　　{"Athens" is plural}

procax　libertas　miscuit　civitatem,　frenumque
an-impudent　freedom　mixed　the-city　and-the-bridle
　　　　(confused)

pristinum　licentia　solvit.　Hic　conspiratis
former　licentiousness　released　Here　having-conspired

partibus　factionum　tyrannus　Pisistratus　occupat
partisans　of-factions　the-tyrant　Pisistratus　occupies

arcem.　Cum　Attici　flerent
the-citadel　When　the-inhabitants-of-Attica　were-bemoaning

tristem　servitutem,　non　quia　ille　crudelis　sed
(their) sad　slavery　not　because　he (was)　cruel　but

quoniam omne onus grave insuetis, et
because every burden (is) heavy for-the-unaccustomed and

coepissent queri, Aesopus tum talem fabellam
they-began to-complain Aesop then such-a fable

rettulit. Ranae, vagantes liberis paludibus,
reported Frogs roaming in-the-free marshes
(told)

magno clamore petierunt ab Iove regem, qui
with-a-great shout asked-for from Jupiter a-king who

vi compesceret dissolutos mores.
with-strength would-restrain (their) dissolute customs

Pater deorum risit atque illis dedit
The-Father of the gods laughed and to-those he-gave

parvum tigillum, quod missum subito
a-small piece-of-wood which (being) sent a-sudden

motu sonoque terruit pavidum genus
with-a-motion and-sound terrified the-fearful species

vadi. Cum hoc iaceret mersum
.of-the-shallow-place When this (log) had-lain immersed

| limo | diutius, | forte | una | tacite | profert |
|---|---|---|---|---|---|
| in-the-mud | for a long time | by-chance | one | tacitly | brings |

| caput | e | stagno | et, | explorato | rege, |
|---|---|---|---|---|---|
| (her) head | out-of | the-pond | and | having examined | the-king |

| cunctas | evocat. | Illae | posito | timore |
|---|---|---|---|---|
| to-all | she-calls-out | They | having-put (aside) | (their) fear |

| certatim | adnatant, | supraque | lignum | petulans |
|---|---|---|---|---|
| eagerly | swim near | and-upon | the-wood | the-petulant |

| turba | insilit. | Cum | quod | omni | contumelia |
|---|---|---|---|---|---|
| crowd | leaps | When | that (thing) | with-all (kind-of) | insult |

| inquinassent | miserunt, | rogantes | alium |
|---|---|---|---|
| they-had-tarnished | they-sent (it back) | imploring-for | another |

| regem | ad | Iovem, | quoniam | esset | inutilis |
|---|---|---|---|---|---|
| king | to | Jupiter, | because | would-be | useless |

| qui | fuerat | datus. | Tum | misit | illis |
|---|---|---|---|---|---|
| the-one-that | had-been | given | Then | he-sent | to-those |

| hydrum, | qui | aspero | dente | coepit | corripere |
|---|---|---|---|---|---|
| a-water-snake | which | with-a-rough | tooth | began | to-snatch-up |

singulas. Frustra fugitant necem inertes;
(them) one-by-one In-vain they-flee-from death without-skill

metus praecludit vocem. Furtim igitur dant
the-fear blocks (their) voice Secretly therefore they-give

Mercurio mandata ad Iovem, ut succurrat
to-Mercury messages to Jupiter in-order-that he-saves

adflictis. Tunc contra Tonans. "Quia
the-distressed Then replies The-Thundering (one) Because

noluistis ferre vestrum bonum," inquit
you-did-not-want to-bear your good (one) he-says

malum perferte." "Vos quoque, o cives,"
the-bad (one) endure You also oh citizens

ait, "hoc sustinete, ne veniat maius
said (Æsop), this (evil) endure lest come a-greater

malum".
evil

# III. Superbus Graculus et Pavo

----

III. Superbus Graculus et Pavo
3 The-Arrogant Jackdaw and the-Peacock

Ne libeat gloriari alienis bonis,
In-order-that-not it-pleases to-boast of-other-people's goods (merits)

suoque potius habitu degere vitam,
and-with-his-own rather appearance pass life

Aesopus hoc exemplum prodidit nobis.
Aesop this example has-put-forth to-us

Tumens inani superbia graculus pinnas
Being-swollen with-empty arrogance a-jackdaw (some) wings

quae deciderant pavoni, sustulit,
which had-fallen-off from-a-peacock he-had-picked up
{pavo3}

seque exornavit. Deinde, contemnens
and himself (with-them) had-adorned Then despising

suos, se immiscuit formoso gregi
his-own (kind) himself intermingled with the-beautiful flock

pavonum, Illi eripiunt pinnas impudenti avi,
of-peacocks These tear-out the-plumes to-the-shameless bird

fugantque rostris. Male mulcatus
and-chase-(it)-away with-(their)-beaks Badly injured

graculus coepit redire maerens ad proprium
the-jackdaw began to-return lamenting to his-own

genus, a quo repulsus sustinuit
kind by which having-been-repulsed he-has-endured

tristem notam. Tum quidam ex illis quos prius
a-sad label Then someone out-of those whom before

despexerat, "si fuisses contentus nostris
he-had-despised (said) if you-had-been content with-our

sedibus, et voluisses quod Natura
residences and you-had-been willing that-what Nature

dederat pati, nec expertus esses illam
had-given to-suffer neither experienced you-were that
(would have)

13

contumeliam, nec hanc repulsam tua calamitas
insult      nor    that    rejection    your   calamity

sentiret".
had-felt

# IV. Canis per Fluvium Ferens Carnem

————

IV. Canis per Fluvium Ferens Carnem
4   A-Dog   through   a-River   Carrying   (a piece of) Meat

Amittit   proprium   merito   qui
Loses   (what is his) own   deservedly   he-who

alienum   adpetit.   Cum   canis,   ferret   per
(what's) someone else's   covets   When   a-dog   carried   through

fluvium   carnem,   vidit   natans   in   speculo
a-river   meat   he-saw   swimming   in   the-mirror

lympharum   suum   simulacrum,   et   putans   aliam
of-the-waters   his-own   image   and   thinking   another

praedam   ferri   ab   altero,   voluit
booty   to-be-carried   by   another (dog)   he-wanted

eripere;   verum   aviditas   decepta   et   cibum
to-snatch-away   however   (his) avidity   was deceived   and   the-food

quem      ore      tenebat    dimisit,    nec    quem
which    in-(his)-mouth    he-held    he-released    nor    (that) which

petebat     adeo     potuit   tangere.
he-sought-for    so-greatly    he-could     touch

# V. Leo et Capella, Ovis et Leo

----

## V. Vacca, Capella, Ovis et Leo
V.  Cow  She-goat  Sheep  and  Lion

Numquam est fidelis societas cum potente. Haec
Never is faithful a society with a-powerful This
(an alliance)

fabella testatur meum propositum. Vacca et
fable attests my purpose A-cow and

capella et ovis patiens iniuriae fuere socii
a-she-goat and a-sheep enduring injustice were partners

cum leone in saltibus. Cum hi cepissent
with a-lion in the-forests When these had-captured

cervum vasti corporis, sic est locutus leo
a-deer of-a-huge body thus is spoken the lion
(has)

partibus factis: "Ego hoc nomine primam
with-the-parts made I by-this name the-first (part)

tollo,   quia   rex   cluo;     secundam,    quia   sum
take   because   king   I-am-called   the-second (part)   because   I-am

consors    tribuetis   mihi;   tum,    quia    plus
(your) partner    you-will-yield   to-me    then,   because    more

valeo,    me   sequetur    tertia;     malo
I-am-strong    me   will follow   the-third (part)    by-an-evil

adficietur     quis   si   quartam    tetigerit".
will-be-afflicted    somebody   if   the-fourth-one   he has touched

Sic   totam   praedam   improbitas    sola   abstulit.
Thus    all    the-booty   the-dishonesty    alone   took-away
            (the dishonest one) for himself

# VI. Ranae ad Solem

————

VI.  Ranae  ad  Solem
6.  The-frogs  at  the-Sun

Aesopus  vidit  celebres  nuptias  furis  vicini
Aesop  saw  the-famous  wedding  of-a-thief  neighboring
{fur2}

et  continuo  incipit  narrare:  Cum  quondam  Sol
and  immediately  begins  to-tell  When  once  the-Sun

vellet  ducere  uxorem,  ranae  clamorem
wanted  to-lead  a-wife  the-frogs  a-cry
(to marry)

sustulerunt  ad  sidera.  Permotus  convicio  quaerit
raised  to  the-stars  Stirred  by-the-outcry  asks

Iuppiter  causam  querellae.  Quaedam  incola
Jupiter  the-cause  of-the-complaint  A-certain  resident

stagni  tum  inquit:  "Nunc  exurit  unus  lacus,
of-the-pond  then  says  Now  he-burns  one  the-lake
(alone)

cogitque    omnes   miseras    arida      sede     emori.
and-compels  all (of us)  miserable  by-the-dry  residence  to-die-off

Quidnam  est  futurum  si   crearit   liberos?"
What-then  is  going-to-be  if  he-produces  children

# VII. Vulpes ad Tragicam Personam

----

**VII. Vulpes ad Tragicam Personam**
7. The-fox to the-Tragic Mask
(theatrical)

**Tragicam personam forte vulpes viderat; quam**
A-tragic mask by-chance a-fox had-seen to-which
{persona4} {subject!}

**postquam verterat huc illuc semel**
after she-had-overturned hither and thither once

**atque iterum: "O quanta species,"**
and again (she spoke) Oh however-great the-appearance

**inquit, "cerebrum non habet!" Hoc illis est**
she-says brain not it-has This to-those is

**dictum quibus honorem et gloriam Fortuna**
said to-whom honor and glory Fortune

**tribuit, communem sensum abstulit.**
has-allotted (but) common sense has-taken-away

# VIII. Lupus et Gruis

----

VIII.  Lupus  et  Gruis
8.    The-Wolf  and  the-Crane

Qui           desiderat        pretium          meriti          ab
(he) Who      desires          a-recompense     of (his) merit  from

improbis,   bis    peccat:  primum  quoniam  adiuvat
wicked-people  twice  sins    first    because   he-helps

indignos,    deinde   quia    abire      impune
unworthy (men)  then   because  to-go-off  without-punishment

iam   potest  non.  Cum   devoratum    os     haereret
already  he-can  not   When   (a) devoured  bone   clinged
     he cannot anymore

fauce       lupi,      victus      magno        dolore
in-the-throat  of-a-wolf  conquered  by-the-great   pain

coepit         singulos          inlicere       pretio
he-begins       the single        to-entice     with-a-reward
              (singuli: all one by one)

ut extraherent illud malum. Tandem
in-order-that they-would-extract that evil Finally

gruis est persuasa iureiurando; credens
the-crane is persuaded by-the-oath believing
(entrusting)

gulae longitudinem colli,
to-the-gullet (of the wolf) the length of-the (her) neck

fecit pericolosam medicinam lupo.
she-made (it) a-dangerous medicine for-the-wolf
(remedy)

Pro quo cum pactum praemium flagitaret,
For which when the-agreed reward she-demanded

"Ingrata es," inquit, "quae nostro ore
Ungrateful you says (the wolf) who out-of-our mouth

caput incolume abstuleris, et mercedem
(your) head unharmed you-have-taken-out and a-wage

postules".
you-request

# IX. Passer Consiliator ad Leporem

----

IX.    Passer    Consiliator  ad  Leporem
9.   The-Sparrow    Adviser    to   the-Hare

Sibi    non   cavere   et   aliis   dare  consilium,
For-oneself  not  to be-careful  and  to-others  give  advice

stultum  esse  ostendamus   paucis  versibus.  Passer
foolish   to-be  we-will-show  with-a-few  verses  A sparrow

obiurgabat  leporem,  oppressum  ab  aquila,  fletus
scolded    a hare    fallen-upon  by  an-eagle  weeping
(laments)

graves   edentem:   "Ubi   est   illa   nota
grave   uttering   Where  is  that  (well) known

pernicitas?"  inquit.   "Quid  ita  cessarunt  pedes?"
swiftness   it says.  What (why)  so  stopped  (your) feet

Dum  loquitur,  necopinum  accipiter  rapit  ipsum,
While  he-speaks  an-unexpected  hawk  snatches  him

questuque　　　vano　　clamitantem　　interficit.
and-with-a-complaint　vain　him-crying-out　(the-hawk) kills

Lepus　semianimus　in　solacium　mortis:　"Qui
The-hare　half-dead　in　solace　of-death　(You) who
　　　　　　　　　(as a)

securus　modo　nostra　mala,　inridebas,　simili
careless　just-now　our　evil　laughed-at　with-a-similar

querella　deploras　tua　fata".
lamentation　you-deplore　your　fates
　　　　　　　　　(fate)

# X. Lupus et Vulpes Iudice Simio

----

X.    Lupus    et   Vulpes     Iudice     Simio
10   (the) Wolf   and   (the) Fox   with-(as)-judge   an-Ape

Quicumque     turpi    fraude   semel      innotuit,
   Whoever    by-an-ugly    fraud     once    has-become-known

etiam    si    verum    dicit,    amittit     fidem.     Hoc
even    if    the-true   he-says    he-loses      faith      This
                                       (credibility)

adtestatur    brevis   Aesopi   fabula.     Lupus    arguebat
   attests     a-short   of Aesop    fable     The-Wolf    accused

vulpem    furti    crimine;    illa    negabat    se    esse
the-fox    of-theft   of-a-crime    she     denied    herself   to be
                         (the fox)

proximam   culpae.   Tunc    iudex    simius    inter    illos
   close      of-guilt    Then    (as) judge   an-ape    between   them

sedit.   Cum    uterque    suam   causam    perorassent,
sat.    When   both-of-them    his     cause    they-had-pleaded

**fertur** **simius** **dixisse** **sententiam:** **"Tu** **non**
it-is-told (that) the-ape said the-sentence You not
(pronounced) (wolf)

**videris** **perdidisse** **quos** **petis;** **Credo** **te**
you-seem to-have-lost those you-seek I-believe you
(the things) (fox)

**subripuisse** **quod** **pulchre** **negas".**
have-stolen that-which you-finely deny

# XI. Asinus et Leo Venantes

----

XI.   Asinus   et   Leo   Venantes
11.   The-Donkey   and   the-Lion   Hunting

Expers          virtutis,      verbis      iactans      gloriam,
He-who-has-not   bravery      with-words   boasting     glory
                {virtus2}

fallit        ignotos,                notis                est
deceives      the-ignorant      (but) to-those-who-know     is

derisui.      Leo      vellet   venari   cum      asello
a-laughing stock   (The) Lion   wanted   to-hunt   with   a-little-donkey

comite.          Contexit      illum      frutice      et
as companion      He-concealed   him      in-a-thicket   and
{comes5}

simul          admonuit      ut      insueta          voce
at-the-same-time   he-suggested   that   by-his-unwonted   voice

terreret          feras.      Ipse      exciperet
he-would-frighten   the-wild-beasts   he himself   he would capture

fugientes. Hic auritulus subito tollit clamorem
them-fleeing Here the-long-eared suddenly raises a-cry
(Now)

totis viribus, novoque miraculo turbat
with-all (his) strength and-by-the-new marvel he-confuses
(and by the unusual)

bestias quae, dum paventes, petunt notos
the-beasts that while terrified seek-for the-known

exitus, adfliguntur leonis horrendo impetu.
exits (but) are-afflicted the-lion's horrible by-the-attack.
(but are struck down) by the lion's horrible attack

Qui postquam caede fessus est, asinum
Who after the-slaughter weary is the-donkey
(The lion, who)

evocat, iubetque vocem premere. Tunc ille
calls and-orders (his) voice to-suppress Then he (donkey)

insolens: "Qualis videtur tibi opera meae
insolent How seems to-you the-works of-my
(seem) (achievements)

vocis?" "Insignis," inquit, "sic ut, nisi
voice Extraordinary he-says so (much) that if (I did) not
(the lion says)

nossem tuum animum genusque, fugissem
know your mind and-kind, I-would-have-fled
(courage)

**simili metu".**

similar  in-fear

# XII. Cervus ad Fontem

----

XII.  Cervus  ad  Fontem
12.   The-Deer   at   the-Fountain


Quae        contempseris,   utiliora        laudatis
Which       you-have-disdained  more-useful  (than) what-is-lauded
(That which)

saepe    inveniri,    haec  narratio  est  testis.  Cum  ad
often    to-be-found  this    story    is   witness  When  at


fontem    cervus  bibisset,    restitit,    et  in  liquore
a-fountain  a-deer  had-drunk  he-stood-firm  and  in  the-liquid

vidit    suam    effigiem.  Dum     ibi      mirans,
he-saw   his-own   figure   While   there   contemplating


laudat     ramosa        cornua    crurumque      nimiam
he-praises  (his) branched  antlers   and-of-(his)-legs  the-excessive


tenuitatem        vituperat.    Subito      conterritus
thinness        he-disparages   Suddenly   (being) frightened

vocibus — by-the-voices
venantum, — of-hunters
per — through
campum — the-field
coepit — he-began

fugere, — to-flee
et — and
levi — with-a-light
cursu — run
canes — the-dogs
elusit. — he-eluded
Silva — The-forest

tum — then
excepit — has-caught
ferum; — the-untamed
in — in
qua — which
retentis — by-the-retained

impeditus — hindered
cornibus — antlers
coepit — he-began
lacerari — to-be-lacerated
saevis — by-the-fierce

morsibus — bites
canum. — of-the-dogs
Tum — Then
moriens — dying
dicitur — it-is-said

edidisse — to-have-raised
hanc — this
vocem: — voice (word)
"O — Oh
infelicem — unhappy
me, — me
qui — who

demum — finally (only)
nunc — now
intelligo — I-understand
quam — how
utilia — useful
mihi — to-me
fuerint — have been

quae — (those) which
despexeram, — I-have-despised
*my legs that I despised*
et — and
quae — those-that
laudaram, — I-have-lauded

quantum — how-much
luctus — mourning
habuerint". — they- have-had (brought)

# XIII. Vulpes et Corvus

----

## XIII.  Vulpes  et  Corvus
13.    The-Fox  and  the-Raven

**Quae        gaudent        se        laudari        subdolis**
Those-who    rejoice    themselves    to-be-praised    with-deceitful

**verbis,    dant    poenas    serae    turpi    paenitentia.**
words    give    penalties    of-a-late    shameful    repentance

**Cum    caseum,    de    fenestra    raptum,    corvus    vellet**
When    a-cheese    from    a-window    snatched    a-raven    wanted

**comesse,        residens        arbore        celsa,        vulpes**
to-eat        sitting        on-a-tree        high        the-fox

**invidit,        deinde    sic    coepit    loqui:    "O    qui,**
saw-(it)-with-envy    thereafter    thus    he-began    to-speak    Oh    who
                                                                        (which)

**corve,    est    nitor    tuarum    pinnarum!    Quantum**
o raven    is    the-splendor    of-your    feathers    How-much

geris     decoris     corpore     et   vultu!   Si   haberes
you-wear    of-elegance    in-(your)-body    and    face    If    you-had

vocem,    nulla     ales      foret    prior".   At   ille,
a voice    no-other   winged creature   would-be    prior    But    he

dum   etiam   vocem   vult   ostendere,      lato
while    also    (his) voice   wants    to-show     with-a-wide-open

ore     emisit    caseum;   quem   celeriter    dolosa
mouth   he-dropped   the-cheese    which     quickly     the-deceitful
{os5}

vulpes    rapuit    avidis    dentibus.   Tum   demum,
fox      caught    with-greedy     teeth     Then     finally

stupor     corvi     deceptus,   ingemuit.
the-stupidity   of-the-raven   (being) deceived   he-groaned

# XIV. Medicus Ex Sutore

----

XIV.　Ex　Sutore　Medicus
14.　Out-of　a-Cobbler　a-Doctor

Cum　malus　sutor　deperditus　inopia　coepisset
When　a-bad　shoemaker　(was) destroyed　by-poverty　he-began

facere　medicinam　　ignoto　　loco　et　venditaret
to-do　　medicine　　(in) an-unknown　place　and　　he-sold
　　　　(work as a doctor)

antidotum　　falso　　nomine.　Verbosis　strophis
an-antidote　by-a-false　　name　　With-verbose　　tricks

adquisivit　famam　　sibi.　　Hic,　　cum　iaceret
he-acquired　　fame　　for-himself　This (man)　when　was-lying

　rex　　urbis　confectus　　gravi　morbo,　eius
the-king　of-the-city　consummated　by-a-serious　disease　him
　　　　　　　　　　　　　　　　　　　　　　　{is2}

experiendi　gratia,　scyphum　poposcit:　dein,
to test　　　　　　　a-cup　　he-required　then

fusa   aqua,   simulans   se   miscere
having-been-poured   water   pretending   himself   to-mix

toxicum   illius   antidoto,   iussit   combibere
a-poison   his   with-the-antidote   ordered   to-drink-all

ipsum,   praemio   posito.   Timore   mortis   ille
it   a-reward   being put   By-the-fear   of-death   he
(the cobbler)

tum   est   confessus,   non   se   factum
then   is   confessed   (that) not   he   had-been-made
(has)   (had become)

medicum   nobilem   ulla   prudentia   artis,   verum
a-doctor   renowned   by-any   knowledge   of-the-skill   but

stupore   vulgi.   Rex   advocata
by-the-stupidity   of-the-people   The-king   (having) called in

contione   haec   edidit:   "Quantae   putatis
an-assembly   these (things)   put-forth   How-much   you-think

vos   esse   dementiae,   qui   vestra   capita   non
you   to-be   of-insanity   (you) who   your   heads   not
{you plural}   (insane)   (lives)

dubitatis   credere   cui   nemo   commisit   pedes
hesitate   to-believe   to-whom   nobody   entrusts   (his) feet
(entrust)

calceandos?" Hoc, dixerim, vere pertinere ad illos
to-be-shod     this   I-would-say   truly   to-pertain   to   those

quorum stultitia impudentiae    est     quaestus.
whose    foolishness   of-impudence     is      the-gain
                                       (constitutes)

# XV. Asinus ad Senem Pastorem

----

| XV. | Asinus | ad | Senem | Pastorem |
|-----|--------|-----|-------|----------|
| 15. | (the) Donkey | to | the-old | Shepherd |

| In | commutando | principatu | pauperes | civium |
|----|------------|------------|----------|--------|
| In | a-changing | (of) leadership | the-poor | of-the-citizens |

| nil | mutant | praeter | nomen | domini. | Id | esse |
|-----|--------|---------|-------|---------|-----|------|
| nothing | change | except-for | the-name | of-the-master | That | to-be |

| verum, | haec | parva | fabella | indicat. | In | prato |
|--------|------|-------|---------|----------|-----|-------|
| true | this | small | fable | indicates | In | a-meadow |

| timidus | senex | pascebat | asellum. | Is, |
|---------|-------|----------|----------|-----|
| a-faint-hearted | old-man | was-taking-to-graze | a-donkey | He |

| subito | clamore | hostium | territus, | suadebat |
|--------|---------|---------|-----------|----------|
| by-a-sudden | shout | of-the-enemies | terrified | urged |

| asino | fugere, | ne | possent | capi. | At | ille, |
|-------|---------|-----|---------|-------|-----|-------|
| the-donkey | to-flee | lest | they-could | be-captured | But | he (the donkey) |

lentus: "Quaeso,     num      putas    binas    clitellas
slow        I-ask     whether  you-think double  pack-saddles

impositurum   victorem    mihi?"    Senex      negavit.
will-be-placed by-the-winner on-me  The-old-man denied

"Ergo,     quid    refert      mea        cui       serviam,
Therefore  what    it-matters  my things  to-whom   I-serve
                               (to-me)

dum      portem   unicas  clitellas?"
as-long-as I-wear  single  pack-saddles

# XVI. Ovis Cervus et Lupus

————

XVI.　Ovis,　Cervus　et　Lupus
16.　The-Sheep　the-Stag　and　the-Wolf

Cum　fraudator　advocat　improbos　homines
When　a-defrauder　calls-in　dishonest　men

sponsum,　non　rem　expedire　expetit,　sed
as-a-warrant　not　a-thing　to-bring-forward　he-seeks　but

ordiri　malum.　Cervus　ovem　rogabat　modium
to-begin　an-evil　A-stag　to-a-sheep　asked-for　a-measure

tritici,　lupo　sponsore.　At　illa,　praemetuens
of-wheat　with-a-wolf　as-a-voucher　But　she　fearing-beforehand

dolum:　"Rapere　atque　abire　semper　lupus
a-trick　To-snatch　and　to-go-away　always　the-wolf

adsuevit;　tu　fugere　veloci　impetu
has-been-used-to　you　to flee　with-a-quick　onset

de conspectu.  Ubi  requiram  vos,  cum
out-of-sight  Where  wiil-I-search-for  you-both  when

dies  advenerit?"
the-day  has come
(of payment)

# XVII. Ovis Canis et Lupus

----

XVII.    Ovis,    Canis  et  Lupus
17.    The-Sheep  the-Dog  and  the-Wolf

Mendaces  solent  luere    poenas    malefici.  Cum
Liars      use-to    pay    the-penalties  of-a-misdeed  When

canis    calumniator    peteret    ab    ove    quem
a-dog    false-accuser    requested    from    a-sheep    to-whom

contenderet    se    commendasse  panem,    panem,
he-contended    himself    to-have-confided          a-bread

lupus      citatus        testis,    non    modo    unum
a-wolf    (being) summoned    (as) witness    not    only    one

adfirmavit    deberi    verum    decem    dixit.    Ovis,
he-affirmed    to-be-owed    but    ten    he said    The-sheep

damnata    falso    testimonio,    quod    non    debebat
condemned  by-a-false    testimony    that what    not    she-did-owe

solvit.　　　Post　paucos　dies　　bidens　　lupum
she-paid-for　After　(a) few　days　the-two-hoof　the-wolf
　　　　　　　　　　　　　　　　　　　(sheep)

iacentem　in　fovea　prospexit.　"Haec,"　inquit,　"merces
lying　　in　a-pit　perceived　This　says-she　reward

fraudis　datur　a　superis".
of-fraud　is given　by　those-above

# XVIII. Mulier Parturiens

----

XVIII.    Mulier    Parturiens
18.       The-Woman  in-Labour

Nemo    libenter    recolit    locum    qui    laesit.
Nobody  willingly   recalls   the-place  which  has-injured

Instante    partu,    mulier    mensibus
Being-imminent  the-giving-birth  a-woman  with-(her)-months
{instans5}      {parttus5}

actis  iacebat    humi,    ciens    flebilis    gemitus.
done   lay    on-the-ground  rousing  lamentable  groans
(over)                   (raising)

Vir    est    hortatus    reciperet    corpus    lecto,
(her) Man  is  exhorted (her)  to-carry-back  (her) body  on-the-bed
       (has)

quo    onus    naturae    deponeret    melius.
by which  the-burden  of-nature  she-would-deposit  better

"Minime    confido,"    inquit,    "illo    loco
Not-in-the-least  I-am-confident  she-says,  in-that  place

posse malum finiri quo initio est
to-be-able (my) misfortune to-be-finished where initially it-is
{quis5} {initium5} (has)

conceptum".
been-conceived

# XIX. Canis Parturiens

----

XIX.   Canis   Parturiens
19.   The-Dog   in-Labour

Blanditiae   hominis   mali   habent   insidias;   quas
The-flatteries   of-a-man   evil   they-have   traps   which
   (of a person)

ut   vitemus,   subiecti   versus   monent.
in-order-that   we-avoid   the-following-below   verses   admonish

Cum   canis   parturiens   rogasset   alteram,   ut
When   a-dog   in-labour   asked   another (dog)   that

fetum   in   eius   tugurio   deponeret,   facile
(her) young   in   her   hut   she-might-deposit   easily

impetravit.   Dein   reposcenti   locum
she-obtained (it)   After-that   to-the-requesting-back   (her) place

preces   admovit,   exorans   breve   tempus
prayers   she-addressed   beseeching (for)   a-short   time

dum      firmiores      catulos      posset      ducere.
while      stronger      whelps      she-could      lead-forth
(during which)

Hoc      quoque      consumpto,      coepit      flagitari
This (time)      also      having-expired      (the owner) began      to-solicit

validius      cubile.      "Si      potueris      esse
with-more-vigour      (her) place-of-rest      If      you-can      be

par      mihi      et      meae      turbae,"      inquit,
a-match      for-me      and      for-my      troop      says (the tenant)

"cedam      loco".
I-will-withdraw      from-the-place

# XX. Famelici Canes

----

XX.  Famelici  Canes
20.  The-hungry  Dogs


Stultum  consilium  non  modo  effectu  caret,  sed
A-silly      plan        not    only    of-effect  is-devoid  but


quoque  mortales  ad  perniciem  devocat.  Corium
also      mortals      to  (their) destruction  summons  A-hide


depressum  in  fluvio  canes  viderunt.  Ut
sunk-down   in   a-river   dogs      saw      In-order-that


possent  comesse  id  extractum  facilius,  aquam
they-could    eat       it  (being) extracted  more-easily  the-water


coepere  ebibere:  sed  rupti  prius  perierunt  quam
they-began  to-drink-up  but  burst  earlier  they-perished  than
                                              (before)

contingerent  quod  petierant.
they-could-touch  that-which  they-strove-for

51

# XXI. Senex Leo, Aper, Taurus et Asinus

----

| XXI. | Senex | Leo, | Aper, | Taurus | et | Asinus |
|------|-------|------|-------|--------|-----|--------|
| 21. | The-old | Lion | the-Wild Boar | the-Bull | and | the-Donkey |

| Quicumque | amisit | pristinam | dignitatem, | etiam | est |
|-----------|--------|-----------|-------------|-------|-----|
| Whoever | lost | (his) former | dignity | also | is |

| iocus | ignavis | in | gravi | casu. | Cum |
|-------|---------|-----|-------|-------|-----|
| a-joke (laughing stock) | for-the-cowards | in | a-grave | case (misfortune) | When |

| defectus | annis | et | desertus | viribus | leo |
|----------|-------|-----|----------|---------|-----|
| worn-out | by-the-years | and | abandoned | by (his) strength | a-lion |

| iaceret, | trahens | extremum | spiritum, | aper |
|----------|---------|----------|-----------|------|
| laid | drawing | (his) final | breath | a-boar |

| fulmineis | dentibus | venit, | et | vindicavit | ictu |
|-----------|----------|--------|-----|------------|------|
| with-lightning | teeth | came | and | avenged | with-a-thrust |

| veterem | iniuriam. | Infestis | cornibus | taurus |
|---------|-----------|----------|----------|--------|
| an-old | wrongdoing | With-hostile | horns | a-bull |

mox    confodit    hostile    corpus.    Asinus,    ut
presently    stabbed    the-hostile    body    The-donkey    when
    (of his enemy)

vidit    ferum    impune    laedi,    calcibus
it-saw    the-wild animal    with-impunity    to-be-injured    with-kicks

frontem    extudit.    At    ille,    exspirans:    "Tuli
(its) front    stroke    But    he    expiring    (said) I-have-borne
    (the lion)

fortis    indigne    insultare    mihi.    Te,    naturae
the-strong-one    indignantly    to-insult    me    You    of nature
    (But you)

dedecus,    quod    cogor    ferre,    bis    videor
disgrace    because    I-am-compelled-to    bear    twice    I-am-seen
    (endure)    (I seem)

mori".
to-die

# XXII. Mustela et Homo

----

XXII.   Mustela   et   Homo
22.   The-Weasel   and   the-Man

Mustela   ab   homine   prensa,   cum
A-weasel   by   a-man   having-been-captured   because

instantem   necem   vellet   effugere,   "Parce   mihi,
an-instant   death   it-wanted   to-escape   Spare   me

quaeso,"   inquit,   "quae   purgo   domum   tibi
please   she-says   (me) who   I-purge   the-house   for-you

molestis   muribus."   Ille   respondit:   "Si   faceres
of-troublesome   mice   He   responds   If   you-did (it)

mea   causa,   esset   gratum   et   dedissem
(for) my   cause   it-would-be   nice   and   I-would-have-given
(sake)

veniam   supplici.   Nunc,   quia   laboras
pardon   to (your) suppliant   (But) now   because   you-work

ut                fruaris        reliquiis     quas     sunt
in-order-that    you-may-enjoy    the-left-overs    which    they are

rosuri,    et       simul           devores      ipsos,
to-gnaw    and    at-the-same-time    you-may-devour    those (mice)

noli     imputare  vanum  beneficium  mihi." Atque
do-not-want    to-ascribe    a-vain       benefit      to-me    And

ita     locutus,      dedit     leto      improbam.    Hoc
thus    having-spoken    he-gave    to-death    the-wicked-one    This

dictum  illi    debent  agnoscere  in      se,      quorum
saying    those    must    acknowledge    to   themselves    whose
                                                 (for)

privata  utilitas    servit      sibi,        et     iactant
private    usefulness    serves    to-themselves    and    boast

inane    meritum  imprudentibus.
an-empty    merit       to-the-unaware

# XXIII. Canis Fidelis

----

XXIII.   Canis   Fidelis
23.   The-Dog  Faithful

Repente      liberalis      est gratus   stultis,
Suddenly   (somebody being) generous   is   nice   for-the-stupid

verum     peritis     tendit    inritos   dolos.
but   for-the-experienced   it-attempts   ineffective   frauds

Cum nocturnus fur misisset   panem   cani,
When   a-nocturnal   thief had-thrown (a piece of) bread   to-a-dog

temptans   an    obiecto   cibo   posset
trying   whether   with-the-thrown   food   he-could

capi,   "Heus",   inquit,   "meam   linguam
captivate (it)   Hey   says (the dog)   my   tongue (mouth)

vis   praecludere, ne latrem pro   re
(do) you-want   to-shut   lest   I-bark   for   the-property

**domini?** **Multum** **falleris.** **Namque** **ista** **subita**
of-the-master Very-much you-err And-since that sudden

**benignitas** **iubet** **me** **vigilare,** **ne**
benignity compels me to-watch that you not

**facias** **lucrum** **mea** **culpa."**
you might make profit through-my fault

# XXIV. Rana Rupta et Bos

----

XXIV.   Rana   Rupta   et   Bos
24.   The-Frog   Burst   and   the-Bull

Inops,   dum   vult   imitari   potentem,   perit.   In
The-weak   while   he-wants   to-imitate   the-strong   perishes   In

prato   quondam   rana   conspexit   bovem,   et
a-meadow   once   a-frog   saw   a-bull   and

tacta   invidia   tantae   magnitudinis   rugosam
touched   by-envy   of-such-a-great   magnitude   (her) wrinkled

pellem   inflavit.   Tum   interrogavit   suos   natos
skin   she-swelled   Then   she-inquired   with-her   offspring

an   bove   esset   latior.   Illi   negarunt.
whether   than-the-bull   she-was   larger   They   said-no

Rursus   intendit   cutem   maiore   nisu,   et
Again   she-stretched-out   (her) skin   with-more   effort   and

simili modo quaesivit, quis esset maior. Illi
in-the-same way she-asked who was greater They

dixerunt "bovem". Novissime indignata, dum
said the-bull At-last (being) offended while

vult validius inflare sese, iacuit
she-wants with-more-vigour to-inflate herself she-lay-down
(it died)

rupto corpore.
with-a-burst body

# XXV. Canes et Corcodilli

----

XXV.   Canes   et  Corcodilli
25.   The-Dogs  and  the-Crocodiles

Qui       dant  prava   consilia   cautis    hominibus
Who       give   crooked   advices   to-cautious   men
(Those who)

et   perdunt   operam   et   deridentur   turpiter.
and   lose   the-effort   and   are-laughed-at   shamefully
(both)

Est   traditum   canes  bibere  in  Nilo  flumine
It-is   handed down   dogs   drink   in   the-Nile   river
(has-been)

currentes,   ne   rapiantur  a  corcodillis.  Igitur,
running   that not  they-be-seized  by  the-crocodiles  Therefore

cum   canis   coepisset   bibere   currens,   sic
when   a-dog   began   to-drink   running   thus

corcodillus:   "Quamlibet  lambe   otio,   noli
(spoke) the-crocodile   As-it-pleases   lick   with-leisure   will-not

vereri". At    ille:    "Facerem,  mehercules,  nisi
fear    But    he    I-would-do (it)  by-Hercules  if-(I)-not
        (the dog said)

scirem  meae  carnis  esse  cupidum  te."
knew    of-my    flesh    to-be    desirous    you

# XXVI. Vulpes et Ciconia

----

XXVI. Vulpes  et  Ciconia
26.      The-Fox  and  the-Stork

Nulli      nocendum:   si    quis   vero    laeserit,
No-one  is-to-be-harmed  if   anyone  truly  has-injured

multandum        simili    iure     fabella
that-he-is-to-be-punished   by-a-similar  law   (this) fable

admonet.  Dicitur  vulpes  ad  cenam  ciconiam  prior
adhorts   It-is-said  the-fox  for  dinner   the-stork   first

invitasse,   et   posuisse  liquidam  sorbitionem  in
to-have-invited  and  to-have-put  a-liquid   broth   in

patulo    marmore   quam   nullo   modo   potuerit
a-wide-open  marble (plate)  which  in-no   way   could

gustare   esuriens   ciconia.  Quae,  cum  revocasset
taste    the-hungry   stork   Who   when  she-re-invited

vulpem,    posuit      lagonam      plenam
the-fox      set     a-bottle-with-narrow-neck     full

intrito    cibo;    ipsa    inserens    rostrum    huic
with-minced    food    she    introducing    (her) beak    into it
                  (the-stork)

satiatur    et    torquet   convivam    fame.    Quae
satiates-herself   and    tortures    the-guest    with-hunger    Who
                                     (The fox)

cum    lagonae    collum    frustra   lamberet,   accepimus
when    the-bottle's    neck    in-vain    she licked    we-learn

sic    locutam    peregrinam    volucrem:    "Quisque
thus    spoken    the-travelling    winged creature    Each

sua    exempla   debet   pati    aequo    animo".
his-own    examples    should   suffer   with-equal    spirit

# XXVII. Canis et Thesaurus et Vulturius

----

XXVII.  Canis   et  Thesaurus  et  Vulturius
27.    The-Dog  and  the-Treasure  and  the-Vulture

Haec  res      avaris      potest  esse  conveniens,  et
This  thing  to-the-avaricious   can     be      convenient     and
      (story)

  qui,    humiles  nati,  student    dici      locupletes.
(those) who  humble   born   desire  to-be-called    wealthy

Effodiens  humana  ossa  canis  invenit  thesaurum,  et,
Digging-up   human   bones  a-dog   finds     a-treasure    and

  quia      violarat        Manes        deos,  iniecta
because   he-had-violated      the-Manes        gods    infused
                        (the-ghosts-of-the-dead) (divine)

est     illi     cupiditas    divitiarum,        ut
is    in-him    a-greed       of-riches     in-order-that

penderet  sanctae  poenas  religioni.  Itaque,  dum
he-would-pay  the-holy  penalties  to-religion  Therefore   while

custodit　aurum,　oblitus　cibi,　est
he-guards　the-gold　having-forgotten　about-the-food　he-is

consumptus　fame.　Super　quem　stans　vulturius
consumed　by-hunger　Above　whom　standing　a-vulture
　　　　　　　　(him)

fertur　locutus:　"O　canis,　merito　iaces
is-reported　(to-have) said　Oh　dog　deservedly　you-lie down

qui　concupisti　subito　regales　opes,
who　have-coveted　suddenly　royal　riches

conceptus　trivio,　educatus
(you) having-been-conceived　at-a-crossroads　brought-up

stercore".
in-a-dunghill

# XXVIII. Vulpes et Aquila

----

XXVIII. Vulpes  et  Aquila
  28.       The-Fox  and  the-Eagle

Quamvis    sublimes,    debent    metuere    humiles,
However       high      they-must      fear      the-humble

  quia    vindicta    patet    docili    sollertiae.
because    revenge   stands-open   to-teachable   ingenuity
                                  (easily taught)

Aquila    quondam    sustulit    vulpinos    catulos,
An-eagle     once    picked-up    vulpine      cubs

  nidoque       posuit       pullis,       ut
and-in-the-nest  she-has-put  for-the-young-ones  so-that

carperent    escam.    Mater    persecuta    hanc
they-should-seize  the-food  The-mother  having-followed  that-one
                                                    (the eagle)

incipit    orare,    ne    tantum    luctum
begins    to-pray   that-not   so-much    mourning

importaret      miserae      sibi.      Illa
she-would-bring-upon    to-the-miserable    to herself    She
                                                        (The eagle)

contempsit,     tuta     quippe     ipso     loco.     Vulpes
scorned (it)     (being) safe     of-course     in-that     place     The-fox

rapuit    ab    ara    ardentem    facem,    totamque
snatched    from    an-altar    a-blazing    torch    and-all
                                                        (the whole)

arborem      flammis      circumdedit,      miscens
tree      with-flames      surrounded      mixing

damno      dolorem      sanguinis      hosti.
with-the-damage      the-sorrow      for-the-blood      for-the-enemy
                                                  (offspring)

Aquila,      ut      eriperet      suos
The-eagle      in-order-that      she-would-rescue      her-own

periculo    mortis,    supplex    reddidit    incolumes
from-the-peril    of-death    as-a-supplicant    gave-back    unharmed

natos    vulpi.
the-children    to-the-fox

# XXIX. Asinus Inridens Aprum

----

XXIX.    Asinus    Inridens  Aprum
29.    The-Donkey  Laughing-at  the Boar

Plerumque   dum   stulti   captant   levem   risum,
Generally   while   the-stupid   captivate   a-light   laughter,
(reckless)

alios   destringunt   gravi   contumelia,   et
other people   they-scour   with-a-serious   insult   and

concitant  nocivum  periculum  sibi.
they-stir-up  a-harmful  danger  to-themselves

Cum  asellus  fuisset  obvius  apro,  "Salve,"  inquit,
When  a-donkey  was  in-the-way-of  a-boar  Hello  (he) said
(encountered)

"frater".  Ille  indignans  repudiat  officium,
brother  He  offended  repudiates  the-courtesy
(The boar)  (refuses to repeat)

et  quaerit  cur  sic  velit  mentiri.  Asinus,
and  asks  why  so  he-liked  to-lie  The-donkey

pene demisso, "Si similem tibi negas me
(his) penis (having) lowered If similar to-you you-deny me

esse, certe simile est hoc tuo rostro."
to-be certainly similar is this-one to-your muzzle

Cum aper vellet facere impetum
Even though the-boar wanted to-make an-attack

generosum, repressit iram et "Vindicta
generous he-repressed (his) wrath and (said) "Revenge

est facilis mihi, sed nolo inquinari
is easy for-me but I-do-not-want to-defile-myself

ignavo sanguine".
with-worthless blood

# XXX. Ranae Metuentes Proelia Taurorum

————

XXX. Ranae Metuentes Proelia Taurorum
30. The-Frogs Fearing the-Battles of-the-Bulls

Humiles laborant ubi potentes dissident.
The-humble take-pains where the-powerful are-at-variance

Rana intuens e palude pugnam taurorum, "Heu,
A-frog looking from a-swamp to-a-fight of-bulls Hey

quanta pernicies instat nobis," ait.
how-much destruction is-at-hand for-us she-said

Interrogata ab alia cur diceret hoc, cum
Questioned by another (one) why she-had-said this because

illi certarent de principatu gregis, longeque
they fought about the-leadership of-the-herd and-far

ab ipsis boves degerent vitam, "Sit separata
from them the-bulls spent (their) life Be-it a-separated

statio ac diversum genus," ait, "qui
living-space and a-different race she said he-who
(the other one said)

expulsus profugerit regno nemoris;
is-expelled flees from-the-kingdom of-the-forest

veniet in secreta latibula paludis et
he will-come in the-secret hiding-places of-the-marsh and

proculcatas obteret duro pede. Ita
the-trampled-upon he-will-crush with (his) hard foot Thus

furor illorum pertinet ad nostrum caput".
the-fury of-those pertains to our head

# XXXI. Milvus et Columbae

----

XXXI. Milvus  et  Columbae
31.   The-Kite  and  the-Pigeons

Qui  committit  se  improbo  homini  tutandum,
Who  commits  himself  to-a-wicked  man  to-be-protected

dum  requirit  auxilia  exitium  invenit.  Cum
while  searches-for  help  destruction  he-finds  When

columbae  saepe  fugissent  milvum,  et  celeritate
the-pigeons  often  fled  the-kite  and  by-the-speed

pinnae  vitassent  necem,  raptor  vertit  consilium
of-wing  avoided  death  the-raptor  turned  advice
(the kite)

ad  fallaciam,  et  decepit  inerme  genus
into  fallacy  and  misled  the-defenseless  race

tali  dolo: "Quare  potius  ducitis  aevum
with-such  deceit  Why  rather  would-you-conduct  a-life

sollicitum quam creatis me regem icto
anxious than you-create me king with-the-stroke
(you make)

foedere, qui praestem vos tutas ab omni
of-a-treaty who shall-stand-before you-all safe from all
(guarantee)

iniuria?" Illae credentes tradunt sese milvo.
injury They believing deliver themselves to-the-kite

Qui adeptus regnum coepit vesci
Who having-obtained the-kingdom begins to-eat

singulas, et exercere imperium saevis
them-one-by-one and to-exercise power with-cruel

unguibus. Tunc una de reliquis
claws Then one of the-remaining-ones (said)

"Merito plectimur, quae spiritum huic
Deservedly we-are-punished (we) who (our) spirit to-this
(our life)

praedoni commisimus".
robber we-have-delivered
{praedo3}

75

# LIBER SECUNDUS - PROLOGUS

----

## Prologus
Prologue

| PHAEDRI | AVGVSTI | LIBERTI | SECVNDVS |
|---|---|---|---|
| OF-PHAEDRUS' | OF-AUGUST | FREEDMAN | THE-SECOND |
| | former slave freed by Augustus | | |

| LIBER | AESOPIARVM | FABVLARVM |
|---|---|---|
| BOOK | OF-AESOPIAN | FABLES |

| Genus | Aesopi | continetur | exemplis; | nec |
|---|---|---|---|---|
| The-kind | of-Aesop | is-contained | in-examples | nor |
| (The literary genre) | | (consists of) | | |

| quicquam | aliud | quaeritur | quam | ut | per | fabellas |
|---|---|---|---|---|---|---|
| anything | else | is-sought | than | that | by | tales |

| corrigatur | mortalium | error, | acuatque | sese |
|---|---|---|---|---|
| be corrected | mortal men's | error | and-he-sharpens | himself |

| diligens | industria. | Quicumque | fuerit | ergo |
|---|---|---|---|---|
| diligently | with-zeal | Whatever | be | therefore |

narrandi iocus, dum capiat aurem et
the-narration's joke as-long-as it-captures the-ear and
(play)

servet suum propositum re commendatur,
serves its purpose by-the-thing it-is-recommended
(subject matter)

non auctoris nomine. Equidem servabo
not by-the-author's name Indeed I-will-preserve

omni cura morem senis. Sed si libuerit
with-all care the-custom of-the-wise man But if it-pleased
(of Aesop)

interponere aliquid dictorum ut
to-interpose something of (my own) statements so-that

varietas delectet sensus, ita velim, lector,
variety may-delight the-senses thus I-would-like reader

accipias in bonas partes, si illi brevitas
that-you-accept in good parts if for-him brevity

rependet gratiam. Cuius ne sit verbosa
recompenses the-favor Of-which that-not-be verbose

commendatio, attende cur debeas negare
the-recommendation consider why you-should deny

**cupidis,** **etiam** **offerre** **modestis,** **quod**
to-the-greedy   and   offer   to-the-modest   that-which

**non petierint.**
they-have-not-asked-for

# I. Iuvencus, leo, et praedator

----

Iuvencus,       leo,    et  praedator
The-young-bull  the-lion  and  the-predator

Super    deiectum    iuvencum  stabat  leo.  Praedator
Over   a-brought-down   young bull    stood   a-lion  A-predator

intervenit  postulans  partem.    "Darem,"       inquit,
intervened    requiring    a-share   I-would-give (it)  (the lion) says

   nisi soleres        sumere      per       te.       Et
if-you-were-not-used        to-take      for     you (alone)    And

improbum        reiecit.      Forte   innoxius  viator
the-wicked       he repels     By-chance  a-harmless  traveller
              (is repelled by the lion)

est  deductus  in  eundem  locum.       Feroque
has    been-led   into   the-same    place    And-by-the-wild-beast

   viso        rettulit   retro  pedem.   Cui
having-been-seen      (he) retraced   retro   his-foot    To-whom

ille,       placidus,     "Non       est     quod      timeas,"
he          amicably    No (thing)  (there) is  that   you-should-fear
(the lion)

ait.     "Et,    pars    quae   debetur    tuae    modestiae,
(he) says   And  the-part  that   is-due    to-your    modesty

audaciter      tolle."     Tunc        diviso          tergore
fearlessly      take        Then    having-divided     the-back
                                                        (the body)

petivit            silvas,       ut      daret      accessum
(the lion) headed-for   the-forests   so-that   he-gives      access

homini.     Egregium     exemplum        prorsus        et
to-the-man   An-egregious     example     straightforward    and

laudabile;   verum    aviditas    est    dives    et    pudor
praiseworthy   truly    avidity     is     rich    and   decency

pauper.
poor

# II. Anus Diligens Iuvenem, Item Puella

----

| Anus | Diligens | Iuvenem, | Item | Puella. |
|---|---|---|---|---|
| An-Old-Woman | Loving | A-Young (man) | Same (So-does) | the-Girl |

| Utcumque | viros | spoliari | a | feminis, |
|---|---|---|---|---|
| One-way-or-another | men | are-robbed | by | women |

| ament, | amentur, | nempe | exemplis |
|---|---|---|---|
| (whether) they-love | (or) are-loved | certainly | by-examples |

| discimus. | Mulier | non | rudis | tenebat | quendam |
|---|---|---|---|---|---|
| we-learn | A-woman | not | inexperienced | held (had) | somebody (a husband) |

| mediae | aetatis | celans | annos | elegantia, |
|---|---|---|---|---|
| of-middle | age | concealing | (her) years | with-elegance |

| animosque | eiusdem | iuvenis | pulchra |
|---|---|---|---|
| and-the-soul | of-the-same (man) | a-young | beautiful-woman |

| ceperat. | Dum | ambae | volunt | videri |
|---|---|---|---|---|
| had-captivated | While (Because) | both-women | they-want | to-seem |

pares     illi,     invicem     coeperunt     legere     capillos
equal     to-him     by-turns     they-begun     to-collect     hairs
(of equal age)

homini,     qui     putaret     se     fingi     cura
from-the-man     Who     imagined     himself     to-be-groomed     by-the-care
{homo3}

mulierum.     Calvus     repente     est     factus;     nam
of-the-women     Bald     suddenly     he-is     made     for

funditus     canos     puella,     nigros
completely     the-grey (hairs)     the-girl     (and) the-black-ones

anus     evellerat.
the-old-woman     had-plucked out

# III. Aesopus ad Quendam de Successu Improborum

————

**Aesopus ad Quendam de Successu Improborum.**
Aesop · to · Somebody · about · the-Success · of-the-Wicked

**Quidam · laceratus · morsu · vehementis**
Somebody · having-been-wounded · by-the-bite · of-a-furious

**canis, misit panem tinctum cruore · malefico,**
dog · threw · bread · dipped · in-blood · to-the-malicious (dog)

**quod · audierat · esse · remedium · vulneris.**
because · he-had-heard · (that) to-be · a-remedy · for-the-wound {vulnus2}

**Tunc sic Aesopus: "Noli · facere hoc coram**
Then · thus · Aesop · Do-not-want · to-do · this · in-front-of

**pluribus · canibus, ne · devorent · nos · vivos · cum**
several · dogs · lest · they-devour · us · alive · when

**scierint · esse · tale · praemium · culpae. · Successus**
they-know · to-be · such · the-reward · of-the-crime · The-success (realize)

improborum   allicit   plures.
of-the-wicked   appeals   (to) many

# IV. Aquila, feles, et aper

----

Aquila,    Feles,   et   Aper.
The-Eagle  the-Cat  and  the-Boar

Aquila    in   sublimi   quercu   nidum   fecerat;   feles
An-eagle  in   a-high    oak      a-nest  had-made   a-cat

    nancta         cavernam   in   media        pepererat;
having-discovered        a-hole     in   the-middle   had-given-birth
                                   {pqp of pario}

sus    nemoris         cultrix           fetum       ad    imam
a-pig  of-the-forest   (female) dweller  (its) young  at   the-bottom
      {nemus2}

posuerat.   Tum    fortuitum        contubernium       feles
had-placed  Then   the-accidental   dwelling-together  a-cat

fraude     et    scelesta   malitia     sic          evertit.    Ad
by-fraud   and   criminal   by-malice   in this way  overturned  To

nidum     volucris       scandit:     "Pernicies,"  ait,        "tibi
the-nest  of-the-bird    she-climbed  Destruction   she-said    for-you

paratur, forsan et miserae mihi; nam quod
is-prepared perhaps also miserable for-me for that
{misera3}

vides insidiosum aprum fodere terram cotidie,
you-see the-insidious boar to dig the-soil daily

vult evertere quercum, ut in plano
he-wants to-overturn the-oak in-order-that in the-flat
(on) (level ground)

facile nostram progeniem opprimat." Terrore
easily our offspring he-may-capture Terror

offuso et perturbatis
(having-been) spread-out and having-been-disturbed

sensibus derepit ad cubile
(the eagle's) senses (the cat) crawled-down to the-bed

setosae suis: inquit "In magno periclo sunt tui
of-the-bristly boar she-says in great peril are your
{sus2}

nati; nam, simul exieris pastum
born for at-the-same-time you-have-gone-out to-the-pasture
(sons) {pastus4}

cum tenero grege, aquila est parata rapere
with the-tender flock the-eagle is ready to-snatch

porcellos tibi." Postquam hunc locum quoque
the-piglets from-you After this place also
{tu3} {hic4}

timore complevit, dolosa condidit sese
with-fear she-has-filled the-cunning (cat) settled herself
{timor5}

tuto cavo. Inde evagata noctu
in-a-safe hole Thence having-wandered-out by-night

suspenso pede ubi esca replevit se et
hung-up by-foot where food (was) she-refilled herself and
on tiptoe on tiptoe

suam prolem, prospicit simulans pavorem toto
her children (and) looked-out pretending fear all

die. Metuens ruinam, aquila desidet ramis;
day Fearing the-fall the-eagle sits-idle on-the-branches;
{dies5}

aper, vitans rapinam, non prodit foras.
the-boar avoiding the-robbery (does) not she-goes-forth outside

Quid multa? Cum suis sunt consumpti
What many? Because the-boar's are consumed
{sus2}

inedia felisque catulis praebuerunt
by-not-eating and-of-the-cat for-the-cubs they-have-offered

largam dapem. Quantum mali saepe
a-large meal (About) how-much of-evil often
{malum2}

concinnet bilinguis homo, stulta credulitas
causes a-two-tongued man the-stupid credulity

potest habere documentum.
can have a-lesson

# V. Caesar ad Atriensem

----

Caesar ad Atriensem.
The-Emperor to the-Steward

Est quaedam natio ardalionum Romae trepide
(there) Is a-certain tribe of-busybodies in-Rome hurriedly

concursans, occupata in otio, gratis anhelans
running-about engaged in leisure gratuitously gasping-at

multa agendo, agens nihil, molesta
many-things to-do (but) doing nothing bothersome

sibi, et aliis odiosissima. Si possum,
to-themselves and to-others very-unpleasant If I-can

hanc emendare tamen volo vera fabella:
this to-correct however I-want with-a-true fable
(this tribe)

est pretium operae attendere.
there-is a-reward for-the-effort of-paying-attention

Caesar Tiberius cum petens Neapolim venisset
The-Emperor Tiberius when going-to Naples had-come

suam villam Misenensem, quae in monte summo
to-his villa Misenian which on a-mountain very high
(at Misenum)

posita Luculli manu. Prospectat Siculum
(was) placed of-Lucullus' by-the-hand it-looks-out at-Sicily
(the architect)

et respicit Tuscum mare. Unus ex
and views-back the-Tyrrhenian Sea One out-of
(on the other side views)

alticinctis atriensibus, cui tunica erat destricta
high-girded stewards to-whom the-tunic was stripped-off
(busy) {quis3}

ab umeris Pelusio linteo, cirris
from the-shoulders with-Pelusian linen with-ringlets

dependentibus, domino perambulante laeta
hanging-down with-the-master walking-around the-joyful

viridia, coepit ligneo alveolo
green (the steward) began with-a-wooden basin
(plants)

conspargere aestuantem humum, come
to-sprinkle the-burnt ground courteous
{comis4ntr}

officiolum     iactitans,    sed     deridetur.     Inde
(his) little-service    boasting     but    he-is-laughed-at    Then

notis    flexibus    praecurrit    in    alium    xystum,
by-known    curves      he-runs     into    another    terrace
        (detours)

sedans     pulverem.    Caesar   agnoscit   hominem
making to settle    the-dust     Caesar    recognizes    the-man

remque      intellegit.       Id       ut
and-his-purpose    understands.      This      that
                    (That is to say)

putavit     esse    nescio    quid   boni.    "Heus!"
(the steward) thought   to-be   I-don't-know   what   of-good    Hey

inquit   dominus.   Ille   enimvero   assilit   alacer   certae
says    the-master    He    indeed    jumps    eager    of-a-sure

donationis   gaudio.   Tum    sic    tanta    est   iocata
gift     by-the-joy    Then    thus    so-much    has    joked

maiestas     ducis:    "Non    multum    egisti    et
the-majesty    of-the-leader    Not     much     you-did    and

opera    nequiquam   perit:   Alapae    mecum    multo
the-effort    vainly      dies    Slaps    with-me    at-much
                         (by me)

**maioris    veneunt.**
more        are sold
(higher price)

# VI. Aquila et cornix

----

Aquila    et  Cornix.
The-Eagle and  the-Crow

Contra    potentes   nemo    est   munitus   satis;   si
Against   the-powerful nobody is    protected  enough  if

vero     accessit   maleficus   consiliator,   quicquid
however  accedes    an-evil     counsellor     whatsoever

vis      et   nequitia   oppugnant,   ruit.        Aquila
strength and  wickedness attack       goes-to-ruin An-eagle

sustulit   in     sublime      testudinem.   Quae,   cum
lifted     into   the-height   a-tortoise    Who     as

abdidisset        corpus     cornea    domo         nec   ullo
she-had-concealed (her) body of-horn   in-a-house   not   by-any

pacto   posset   laedi     condita.      Venit   per       auras
pact    could    be-hurt   being hidden  Came    through   the-airs
(means)

cornix et propter volans: "Sane opimam
a-crow and nearby flying (said) Indeed an-abundant

praedam rapuisti unguibus; sed nisi tibi
prey you-snatched with-your-claws however if-not to-you

monstraro quid sit faciendum, nequiquam te
I-show what is to-be-done vainly you
{tu4}

lassabit gravi pondere." Promissa
it-will-wear-out by-the-heavy weight Having-been-promised

parte, suadet ut super scopulum ab
a-share (the crow) persuades that on a-rock from

altis astris illidat duram corticem, qua
the-high stars she-would-break the-hard shell which

comminuta facile vescatur cibo.
having-been-crushed easily (the eagle) would-eat the food

Inducta aquila paruit vafris monitis,
Having-been-induced the-eagle obeyed to-the-sly instructions
{vafer5pl}

et simul divisit magistrae large
and at-the-same-time she-shared with-the-teacher liberally

dapem.    Sic    quae    tuta    fuerat    naturae    munere,
the-meal    So    (she) who    safe    was    of-nature    by-the-gift
{munus5}

occidit    tristi    nece,    impar    duabus.
she kills    with-a-sad    death    not-equal    to-two
{nex2}    not a match

# VII. Duo Muli et Latrones

----

Muli  Duo  et  Latrones.
Mules  two  and  the-Robbers

Gravati  sarcinis  ibant  duo  muli: unus  ferebat  fiscos
Laden  with-bags  went  two  mules  one  carried  baskets

cum  pecunia,  alter  saccos  multo  hordeo
with  money  the-other  bags  with-a-lot  (of) barley

tumentes.  Ille  dives  onere  cervice
swelling  The-former  rich  by-the-burden  with-its-head

eminens  celsa,  clarumque  iactans  collo
standing-out  high  and-clear  boasting  in-the-neck
(held up)  (and loudly)

tintinnabulum,  comes  sequitur  quieto  et
a-bell  the-companion  follows  with-quiet  and

placido  gradu.  Subito  latrones  ex  insidiis
placid  step  Suddenly  thieves  from  an-ambush

advolant    interque    caedem    ferro    sauciant
run-near    and-among    the-carnage    with-iron    wound
                                                              (a sword)

mulum.    Diripiunt    nummos,    neglegunt    vile
a-mule    They-grab    the-coins    they-ignore    the-inexpensive

hordeum.    Cum    spoliatus    casus    igitur
barley    When    the-robbed (one)    having-fallen    therefore

fleret    suos,    "Equidem,"    inquit    alter,    "me
weeps    his things    Certainly    says    the-other    me
(bemoans)    (the money)                                            {ego4}

gaudeo    contemptum,    nam    nil    amisi    nec
I rejoice    having-been-spurnt    for    nothing    I-have-lost    nor

sum    laesus    vulnere."    Hoc    argumento    hominum
I-am    injured    by-a-wound    With-this    argument    men's

tenuitas    est    tuta;    periculo    opes    sunt    magnae
poverty    is    safe    in-peril    riches    are    of-great

obnoxiae.
of-a-handicap

# VIII. Cervus ad Boves

----

**Cervus ad Boves.**
The-Deer  at  the-Oxen

| Cervus | nemorosis | latibulis | excitatus, | ut |
|---|---|---|---|---|
| A-deer | in-the-woody | hideouts | (being) roused | in-order-that |

| effugeret | venatorum | instantem | necem, |
|---|---|---|---|
| he-escaped | of-the-hunters | impending | death |

(by the hands of the hunters)

| caeco | timore | petit | proximam | villam | et |
|---|---|---|---|---|---|
| with-blind | fear | runs-towards | the-next | farm | and |

| condidit | se | opportuno | bovili. | Hic | bos |
|---|---|---|---|---|---|
| hides | himself | in-a-convenient | stall-for-oxen | Here | an-ox |

| latenti: | "Quidnam | voluisti | tibi, |
|---|---|---|---|
| to-the-hiding (says) | What | did-you-want | for-you |

| infelix, | qui | ultro | ad | necem |
|---|---|---|---|---|
| oh unhappy | who | of-your-own-accord | towards | death |

| | | | |
|---|---|---|---|
| **cucurreris** | **hominumque** | **tecto** | **spiritum** |
| you-have-run | and of men {homo2pl} | to-the-roof | (your) spirit (your life) |

| | | | | | | |
|---|---|---|---|---|---|---|
| **commiseris?"** | **At** | **ille** | **supplex:** | **"Vos** | **modo,"** | **inquit,** |
| have-entrusted | But | he | suppliant | You (all) | only (just) | he-says |

| | | | |
|---|---|---|---|
| **"parcite,** | **erumpam** | **occasione** | **data** |
| spare (me) | I-will-rush-out | with-the-opportunity | (being) given |

| | | | | |
|---|---|---|---|---|
| **rursus."** | **Spatium** | **noctis** | **diei** | **excipiunt** |
| again | The-space | of-the-night | of-the-day | follow |

| | | | | | |
|---|---|---|---|---|---|
| **vices.** | **Bubulcus** | **frondem** | **affert,** | **ideo** | **nil** |
| in-turn (each other) | The-herdsman | foliage | brings up | thus | nothing |

| | | | | | |
|---|---|---|---|---|---|
| **videt.** | **Rustici** | **subinde** | **eunt** | **et** | **omnes** |
| (he) sees | The-farm-people | constantly | go | and | they-all |

| | | | | |
|---|---|---|---|---|
| **redeunt,** | **nemo** | **animadvertit.** | **Etiam** | **vilicus** |
| return | nobody | perceives (it) | Also | the-steward |

| | | | | | |
|---|---|---|---|---|---|
| **transit,** | **nec** | **ille** | **quicquam** | **sentit.** | **Tum** |
| passes-by | and-also-not | he | anything | notices | Then |

| | | | | |
|---|---|---|---|---|
| **gaudens** | **ferens** | **ferus** | **bubus** | **coepit** |
| rejoicing | the-enduring | wild (animal) | to-the-oxen {bos3pl} | begins |

agere gratias, quod hospitium praestiterint
to-say thanks because shelter they-had-provided

adverso tempore. Respondit unus: "Salvum
in-an-adverse time Responds one (of-them) Safe

cupimus te quidem; sed si ille venerit, qui
we-want you indeed but if he had come who

centum oculos habet, in magno periculo tua vita
one-hundred eyes has in great peril your life

vertetur. Inter haec dominus ipse a
would-turn While this the-master himself from
(this was being said)

cena redit et quia viderat nuper boves
dinner returns and because he-had-seen lately the-oxen

corruptos, accedit ad praesepe: "Cur
in-bad-condition approaches to the-stall Why

frondis est parum, stramenta desunt?
of-the-foliage there is few the-littering absent

Tollere haec aranea quantum est laboris?" Dum
To-remove these cobwebs how-much it-is of-effort While

scrutatur  singula,  alta  cornua
he-searches  every-single-thing  the-high  horns (antlers)

cervi  quoque  conspicatur;  quem,
of-the-deer  also  are noticed  which (the deer)

convocata  familia,  iubet  occidi
(having) called-in  the-household  he-orders  to-be-killed

praedamque  tollit.  Haec  fabula  significat
and-the-quarry  takes-away  This  fable  means

dominum  videre  plurimum  in  suis  rebus.
the-master  to-see  the-most  in  his own  affairs

# IX. Auctor

----

## Auctor.
The-author

**Aesopi**     **ingenio**     **statuam**     **posuerunt**
To-Aesop's     genius     a-statue     placed

**Attici,**     **servumque**     **collocarunt**
the-inhabitants-of-Attica     and-a-slave     they-placed
(the Athenians)     (one who had been a slave)

**in**   **aeterna**   **basi,**    **ut**    **cuncti**   **scirent**
on   an-eternal   pedestal   in-order-that   all   would-know

**patere**   **viam**   **honoris,**   **gloriam**   **nec**   **generi**
to-be-open   the-path   of-honor   (and) glory   and not   by-race

**tribui,**   **sed**   **virtuti.**   **Quoniam**   **alter**
to-be-conferred   but   by-virtue   Given-that   another
(somebody else)

**occuparat**     **ut**     **primus**     **foret,**
occupies     that     the-first     he-would-be

studui     quod     superfuit:
I (Phaedrus)-have-applied-myself     (to) that-what     remained

ne    solus    esset;    nec   est   haec   invidia,
that-not    the-only-one    he-would-be    and-not   is   this   envy

verum   aemulatio.   Quod   si      Latium
but    emulation    Because   if      Latium
         (the Latin-speaking community)

faverit    meo   labori,    plures    habebit    quos
would-favour   my   effort    more    it-will-have    whom
       (more authors)

opponat    Graeciae.   Si   livor   voluerit,   obtrectare
it-may-oppose   to-Greece   If   ill-will   would-like   to-belittle

curam,     non     eripiet     tamen
(my) diligence     not     it-will-snatch-away     however

conscientiam     laudis.    Si    nostrum    studium
the-consciousness    of-the-praise   If    our    effort

pervenit   ad    tuas   aures   et   animus    sentit
reaches    to    your   ears    and   the-soul   is-sensible-to

arte    fictas    fabulas,   omnem   querelam   felicitas
with-skill   invented   fables    every   complaint   happiness
         {subject}

submovet. Sin autem doctus labor occurrit
removes If however the-learned labor meets

illis quos sinistra natura extulit
with-those whom an-unfavourable nature has-brought-forth

in lucem, nec possunt quicquam nisi carpere
into the-light nor they-can anything if-not to-criticize
(but)

meliores, feram fatale exitium durato
the-better-ones I-will-bear the-fatal ruin with-a-hardened

corde, donec Fortunam pudeat sui criminis.
heart until Fortune feels-shame of-her crime

# LIBER TERTIUS - PROLOGUS

----

## Prologus
Prologue

Phaedri libellos legere si desideras, uaces
Phaedrus booklets to-read if you-wish (that) you-be-free

oportet, Eutyche, a negotiis, ut liber
it-is-necessary Eutychus from affairs so-that (your) free

animus sentiat uim carminis.
soul feels the-force of-the-poem

"Verum", inquis, "non est tanti tuum ingenium,
But you-say not (it) is so much your genius

ut momentum horae pereat meis officiis.
so-that a-moment of-an-hour perishes to-my pursuits

Non ergo causa est id tangi
Not therefore a-cause (there) is (for) it to-be-touched

tuis     manibus,     quod     occupatis     auribus     non
with-your     hands     which     for-engaged     ears     not

conuenit.
(is) suited

Fortasse     dices:     "Aliquae     uenient feriae,     quae
Perhaps     you-will-say     Some-other     come     holidays     that
                                   holidays come

me     soluto     pectore ad studium uocent."
me     with-a-relieved     heart     to     study     call
                      call to study

Legesne,     quaeso,     potius     uiles     nenias,
Don't-you-read     rather     more     worthless     little-tunes

impendas curam quam rei domesticae,     reddas
you-pay     attention     than     case     to-a-domestic     give
      than you pay attention to a domestic matter

amicis     tempora,     uxori     uaces,
to-friends     time     for-the-wife     be-free
                   take some time for your wife

animum relaxes,     otium des corpori,     ut
the-spirit     relax     leisure     give     to-the-body     so-that
    relax your spirit        give leisure to the body

adsuetam fortius praestes uicem?
customary     stronger     excel     duty

Mutandem est propositum tibi ut genus
Change    is    a-goal    for-you    just-as    (your) kind

vitae, si cogitas intrare limen Musarum.
of-life   if   you-think (of)   to-enter   the-threshold   of-the-Muses

Ego, quem Pierio iugo mater enixa
I    whom    in-the-Pierian    summit    (my) mother    brought-forth

est in quo sancta Mnemosyne peperit
is   in   which   the-holy   Mnemosyne   begot
(has)

tonanti Iovi novies fecunda artium
for-the-thundering   Jupiter   nine-times   the-fruitful   arts'

chorum, quamvis paene sim natus in ipsa schola
choir   although   almost   I-am   born   in   the-very   school

curamque habendi penitus corde
and-the-concern   of-possessing   deeply   in-(my)-heart

eraserim et incubuerim invicta laude in
I-have-eradicated   and   inclined   with-invincible   praise   in

hanc vitam, fastidiose tamen in coetum
this   life   fastidiously   however   in   the-assembling

recipior.
I-am-received

Quid    credis    accidere,    illi    qui    quaerit
What    (do) you-think    happens    to-that    who    seeks

exaggerare    magnas    opes    omni    vigilia,
to-enlarge    great    wealth    in-all (while)    awake

praeponens    dulce    lucrum    labori    docto?
preferring    the-sweet    profit    to-the-labor    of-learning

Sed    iam,    "quodcumque    fuerit,"    ut    dixit    Sinon    ad
However    now    whatever-it    (may) be    as    said    Sinon    to

regem    Dardaniae    cum    perductus    foret,    exarabo
the-king    of-Dardania    when    brought-in    he-was    I-will-cultivate

tertium    librum    Aesopi    stilo,    dedicans    illum
the-third    book    with-Aesop's    stylus    dedicating    it
                                      (pen)

tuis    honori    et    meritis.
to-your    honor    and    merits

Quem    si    leges,    laetabor;    sin    autem,    minus
Which    if    you-read    I-will-be-glad    if-not    however    at-least

posteri
the-descendents
certe
certainly
habebunt
will-have
quo
it
oblectent
to-entertain

se.
themselves

Nunc,
Now
fabularum
of-fables
cur
why
sit
would-be
inuentum
invented
genus,
the-genre

breui
briefly
docebo.
(I) will show
Seruitus
Slavery
obnoxia,
indebted
quia
because
non
(it did) not

audebat
dare
dicere
to-say
quae
what
uolebat,
wished
affectus
feelings
proprios
(their) own
in
in

fabellas
fables
transtulit,
transferred
calumniamque
and-the-trickery
elusit
eluded
fictis
with-fictitious

iocis.
games

Ego
I
feci
did
viam
a-road
porro
moreover
illius
(than) this
semita,
foot-path
et
and

cogitavi
I-have-thought
plura
more
quam
than
reliquerat,
remained
deligens
selecting

quaedam in meam calamitatem. Quod si
some in my calamity Because if

accusator foret alius Seiano, si testis
the-prosecutor had-been other than-Sejanus if the-witness

alius, iudex alius denique, faterer me esse
other the-judge other and-finally I-confessed myself to-be

dignum tantis malis, nec delenirem dolorem
deserving so-many woes nor (should) I-soften the-pain

his remediis.
with-these remedies.

Si quis errabit sua suspicione et rapiet
If anyone will-err in-his (own) suspicion and will-snatch

ad se quod erit commune omnium, stulte
to himself what will-be common to-all foolishly

nudabit animi conscientiam. Huic velim
he-will-uncover (his) soul's consciousness To-him I-would-like

me excusatum nihilo minus:
myself (to be) excused by-nothing less

**Enim** **neque** **est** **mens** **mihi,** **notare** **singulos**
For nor is intention for-me to-remark individuals

**verum** **ostendere** **vitam** **ipsam** **et** **mores**
but to-expose life itself and the-habits

**hominum.** **Aliquis** **dicet** **fors** **me** **professum**
of-men Someone says perhaps I (am) devoted

**gravem** **rem.**
to-a-heavy matter

**Si** **Phryx** **Aesopus** **potuit,** **si** **Anacharsis** **Scythes**
If Phryx Aesop could if Anacharsis Scythian

**aeternam** **famam** **condere** **ingenio** **suo,** **ego**
eternal fame build (with) genius his I

**litteratae** **qui** **sum** **proprior** **Graeciae,** **cur** **somno**
to-the-lettered who am nearer Greece why in-sleep

**inerti** **deseram** **patriae** **decus?** **Cum**
incompetent would-desert the-country's glory When

**Threissa** **gens** **numeret** **suos** **auctores,** **Linoque**
the-Thracian race numbers its authors and-to-Linus

Apollo sit parens, Musa Orpheo, qui saxa
Apollo is parent a-Muse (of) Orpheus who rocks

cantu mouit et domuit feras Hebrique
with-(her)-song moves and tamed beasts and-Hebrus'

tenuit impetus dulci mora?
held impetus with-a-sweet delay

Ergo hinc abesto, Liuor, ne frustra gemas,
Therefore from-here be-away envy not in-vain groan

quoniam mihi dabitur sollemnis gloria.
because to-me is-due the-customary glory

Induxi te ad legendum; peto reddas mihi
I-have-induced you to read I-beg you-give me

sincerum iudicium noto candore.
a-sincere judgement with-(your)-well-known candor

# I. Anus ad Amphoram

---

I.    Anus    ad Amphoram
The-old-woman  to  the amphora

Anus    iacere vidit  epotam  amphoram, adhuc
An-old woman  to lay  saw  an-emptied   jar   still
(laying)

Falerna    faece,    quae   e   testa  nobili
Falerner-wine  with the sediment  which  from  pottery  noble

odorem iucundum  late  spargeret.
a scent  pleasant  far and wide  spread

Hunc    postquam   totis  avida    traxit
That (odor)  after  whole  avid  she has inhaled
    wide-open

naribus:  "O suavis anima! Quale in te  dicam
(with) nostrils  O  sweet  breeze  How  in  you  I would say

bonum  antehac   fuisse,   tales  cum  sint
a good thing  before  to have been  such  when  are

reliquiae!"
the remainders

Hoc   quo   pertineat   dicet   qui   me   noverit.
This   to what    applies    may say   who   me   has known

# II. Panthera et Pastores

----

II. Panthera   et   Pastores
The Leopard   and   the Shepherds


Solet  a        despectis        par     referri    gratia.
tends  by  those-held -in-contempt  equal  to be returned  kindness


Panthera inprudens olim  in  foveam  decidit.
A leopard   imprudent   once  into  a pitfall  fell down
                                              {pf}

Viderunt     agrestes;     alii  fustes  congerunt,   alii
saw (her)   the countrymen  others  sticks    brought     others
  {pf}                      some

onerant      saxis;      quidam      contra      miseriti
loaded (it)   with rocks    some      conversely    pitied


          periturae        quippe,     quamvis      nemo
by-her-that-was-to-perish   obviously    although    nobody


laederet,  miserunt  panem      ut       sustineret
she hurt     sent      bread    in order that   it would sustain
           threw down

**spiritum.**
(her) spirit
life

| Nox | insecuta | est; | abeunt | securi | domum, |
|-----|----------|------|--------|--------|--------|
| The night | followed | is<br>has | they go away | confident | home |

| quasi | inventuri | mortuam | postridie. |
|-------|-----------|---------|------------|
| as if<br>supposing | they-were-to-find (her) | dead | on-the-morrow |

| At | illa, | vires | ut | refecit | languidas, |
|----|-------|-------|-----|---------|-----------|
| But | she | (her) strength<br>{pl} | as soon as | she restored<br>{pf} | languid<br>weak |

| veloci | saltu | fovea | sese | liberat | et | in |
|--------|-------|-------|------|---------|-----|-----|
| quick | with a jump | from the pit | herself | frees | and | to |

| cubile | concito | properat | gradu. |
|--------|---------|----------|--------|
| (her) den | rapid | hastens | with step |

| Paucis | diebus | interpositis | provolat, | pecus |
|--------|--------|--------------|-----------|-------|
| A few | days | having passed by | she rushes forward | the sheep |

| trucidat, | ipsos | pastores | necat, | et | cuncta |
|-----------|-------|----------|--------|-----|--------|
| she slaughters | themselves | the shepherds | she kills | and | everything |

| vastans | saevit | irato | impetu. |
|---------|--------|-------|---------|
| devastating | she rages | angry | with fury |

Tum   sibi   timentes   qui   ferae
Then   for themselves   fearing   (those) who   the wild animal

pepercerant   damnum   haut   recusant,   tantum   pro
had spared   the loss   not   object to   only   for

vita   rogant.
(their) life   beg

At   illa:   "Memini   quis   me   saxo   petierit,
But   she (says)   I remember   who   me   with a rock   has gone after

quis   panem   dederit;   vos   timere   absistite;   illis
who   bread   has given   you   to fear   refrain from   to those
  {imp}

revertor   hostis   qui   me   laeserunt."
I come back   (as) an enemy   who   me   have injured

# III. Aesopus et Rusticus

----

III. Aesopus  et  Rusticus
Aesopus    and  the Peasant

Usu             peritus         hariolo           veracior
by practice     expert          than a fortune teller   more truthful

vulgo      perhibetur;  sed    causa    non    dicitur,
by the people   it is asserted   but    the reason   not    is said
generally

quae  nunc  primum     notescet      fabella  mea.
which   now    first    becomes known   by fable    my

Habenti     cuidam      pecora,      oves     perpererunt
Having     for someone    sheep,      the ewes   have brought forth

agnos   humano      capite.      Monstro      territus   ad
lambs    human     with a head   by the monster   terrified    to

consulendos       hariolos      currit  maerens.
to-be-consulted  the fortune tellers   he ran      wailing
{aci}

Hic　　　respondet　pertinere　ad　domini　caput,
This one　　answers　　(it) to pertain　to　of the master　the head

et　avertendum　　victima　　periculum.
and　is-to-be-averted　with a sacrifice　the danger

Ille　　　　autem　adfirmat　significari　coniugem　esse
He　　　　however　affirms　to be meant　(his wife) to be　to be
(another ft)　　　　　　　　　　　　　　　is　　(is)

adulteram　et　insitivos　liberos,　sed　expiari
adulterous　and　spurious　the children　but　be expiated

posse　maiore　hostia.
can　　greater　by a sacrifice

Quid　　multa?　　Variis　　dissident　sententiis,
Why　　many (words)　varying　they disagree　by opinions

hominisque　curam　　maiore　　cura　adgravant.
of the man　the worry　with a greater　worry　they aggravate

Aesopus　ibi　　stans,　　naris　　emunctae
Aesopus　there　(while) standing　(his) nose　having blown

senex,　　cui　　natura　numquam　verba　potuit
an old man　to whom　nature　never　words　could
　　　　　　　　　　　　　　　　　{pf}

dare, "Si procurare vis ostentum, rustice",
give If to take care of you want the prodigy o peasant

inquit "uxores da tuis pastoribus."
he said wives give to your shepherds

# IV. Lanius et Simius

----

IV. Lanius et Simius
The Butcher and the Monkey

Pendere ad lanium quidam vidit simium inter
To hang at the butcher's someone saw an ape among
hanging {pf}

reliquas merces atque opsonia; quaesivit
the remaining merchandise and side-dishes he enquired
(other) {merxpl} {pf}

quidnam saperet.
like what it would taste

Tum lanius iocans "Quale" inquit "caput est,
Then the butcher joking such as said the head is

talis praestatur sapor."
such presents itself the savor

Ridicule magis hoc dictum quam vere aestimo;
Ridiculous more this saying than truly I estimate

quando   et   formosos   saepe   inveni   pessimos,   et
when   and   handsome   often   I have found   the worst   and
(since)   (both)

multos   turpi   facie   cognovi   optimos.
many men   with an ugly   face   I have known   (to be) the best

# V. Aesopus et Petulans

----

V. Aesopus  et  Petulans
Aesopus    and  the Insolent

Successus ad    perniciem    multos    devocat.
Success      to  (their) destruction  many people    lures

Aesopo    quidam petulans lapidem impegerat.
at Aesopus  Someone    insolent    a stone      had thrown
                                                {impingoplupf}

"Tanto"  inquit  "melior!"  Assem  deinde    illi    dedit.
So much   he said  the better  A penny    then    to him    he gave
                                                          {pf}

 Sic    prosecutus: "Plus  non  habeo  mehercule,  sed
Thus    he proceeded    More    not    I have    by Hercules    but
              {pf}

  unde    accipere possis monstrabo tibi.
from where    receive    you can    I will show    to you

Venit    ecce    dives    et    potens;    huic
comes    See    a rich    and    powerful (man)    at that one

similiter impinge lapidem, et dignum
in like manner throw a stone and a worthy

accipies praemium."
you will receive award

Persuasus ille fecit quod monitus fuit, sed
(Being) persuaded he did what advised had been but
{pf}

spes fefellit impudentem audaciam; nam
hope deceived (his) impudent boldness for

comprehensus poenas persolvit cruce.
apprehended the penalties he paid at the cross

# VI. Musca et Mula

----

VI. Musca  et  Mula
The Fly  and  the Mule

Musca        in      temone  sedit   et   mulam  increpans
A (horse)fly  inside  a carriage   sat    and   the mule   reproving
                                  {pf}

"Quam    tarda      es"      inquit   "non      vis        citius
How       slow     you are    it said    not    you want    faster

progredi?
advance

Vide       ne      dolone        collum    conpungam  tibi."
See      that not  with (my) sting  (your) neck  I will puncture   to you
take care

Respondit   illa:   "Verbis   non     moveor     tuis;    sed
Answered     she    By words    not   I am moved    your     but
   {pf}

istum    timeo   qui     sella     prima   sedens   cursum
that one   I fear   who   (in the) seat    first    sitting    running

meum flagello temperat lento, et ora
my with a scourge regulates slow and (my) mouth

frenis continet spumantibus. Quapropter
with bridles holds foaming Therefore

aufer frivolam insolentiam; nam et ubi
desist from silly insolence for and where
{imp} both

tricandum et ubi sit currendum scio."
to dally and where is to to run I know
{ger} should {ger}

Hac derideri fabula merito potest qui
Through this be laughed at fable deservedly can who
may

sine virtute vanas exercet minas.
without strength vain uses threats

# VII. Lupus ad Canem

----

VII.   Lupus   ad   Canem
The Wolf   to   the Dog

Quam   dulcis   sit   libertas   breviter   proloquar.
How   sweet   is   liberty   shortly   I will pronounce
       (be)

Cani   perpasto   macie   confectus   lupus   forte
a dog   well-fed   by meagerness   worn out   A wolf   by chance

occurrit.   Deinde,   salutati   invicem   ut
runs into   Thereupon   (having) greeted   each other   while

restiterunt,"   Unde   sic,   quaeso,   nites?   Aut
they stood still   From where   thus   I ask   you shine?   Or
 {restopf}   how

quo   cibo   fecisti   tantum   corporis?   Ego,   qui
by which   food   have you made   so much   body   I   who
     built up

sum   longe   fortior,   pereo   fame."
am   by far   stronger   I perish   from hunger

Canis    simpliciter:    "Eadem    conditio    est    tibi,
The dog    simply    The same    condition    is    for you
(holds)

praestare    domino    si    par    officium    potes."
perform    for the master    if    an equal    a job    you can

"Quod?"    inquit    ille.    "Custos    ut    sis    liminis,
Which (one)    said    he    a custodian    that    you be    of the entrance

et    a    furibus    tuearis    noctu    domum.    Adfertur
and    from    thieves    you guard    at night    the house    is brought
against

ultro    panis;    de    mensa    sua    dat    ossa
moreover    bread    from    table    his own    gives    the bones

dominus;    frusta    iactat    familia,    et    quod    fastidit
the master    the morsels    throws    the family    and    which    dislikes

quisque    pulmentarium.    Sic    sine    labore    venter
anybody    the meat mix    Thus    without    hard work    belly

impletur    meus."
is filled    my

"Ego    vero    sum    paratus.    Nunc    patior    nives
I    Truly    am    ready (for it)    Now    I suffer    the snows

imbresque in silvis asperam vitam trahens.
and rains in the woods harsh a life leading

Quanto est facilius mihi sub tecto vivere, et
How much it is easier for me under a roof to live and

otiosum largo satiari cibo!"
at leasure bountiful to be satisfiwed with food

"Veni ergo mecum." Dum procedunt, aspicit
Come therefore with me While they go on looks at

lupus a catena collum detritum cani.
the wolf by the chain the neck (being) worn out for the dog

"Unde hoc, amice?" "Nil est." "Dic, sodes,
Wherefrom that my friend Nothing it is Tell (me) please

tamen."
nevertheless

"Quia videor acer, alligant me interdiu,
Because I seem fierce they tie up me during the day

luce ut quiescam, et vigilem
while it is light in order that i be silent and that I keep watch

nox    cum    venerit.    Crepusculo    solutus    qua
the night    when    has come    at dusk    (I am) unleashed    where

visum    est    vagor."
seemed    it has    I wander

"Age,    abire    si    quo    est    animus,    est
Allright    to go away    if    (tom go) wherever    is    the mood    there is

licentia?"
permission

"Non    plane    est"    inquit.    "Fruere    quae    laudas,
Not    quite    there is    he says    Enjoy    what    you praise

canis;    regnare    nolo    ut    liber    non    sim
dog    to rule    I do not want    so that    free    not    I may be

mihi."
for myself

# VIII. Soror ad Fratrem

----

VIII.   Soror   ad  Fratrem
The sister  to   the Brother

Praecepto       monitus      saepe        te        considera.
by (this) advice    warned       often     you(rself)     look at
{imp}

Habebat   quidam    filiam     turpissimam,   idemque
had       Somebody   a daughter    very ugly      and same
also

insignem  pulchra    facie     filium.
noteworthy  handsome  for (his) face   a son

Hi     speculum, in cathedra    matris    ut   positum
These    a mirror   in   the seat  of the mother  as    placed
they                                        where

fuit,    pueriliter ludentes   forte   inspexerunt.
it had been  childishly   playing   by chance   looked into
{pf}

Hic   se    formosum   iactat;  illa  irascitur    nec
He    himself   handsome    he boasts  she   is angry    and not

gloriantis   sustinet    fratris    iocos,   accipiens
bragging     stands   of (her) brother  the jokes   taking

(quid   enim?)  cuncta  in  contumeliam.
what (else)  indeed  everything  in   an insult
                               as

Ergo    ad   patrem   decurrit  laesura  invicem,
Therefore  to  (her) faither  ste runs  to injure  in turn
                                  {futinf}

magnaque  invidia criminatur filium,   vir    natus,
and with great  jealousy  she accuses  the son  (as a) man  born

quod  rem  feminarum tetigerit.
that  a thing  of the ladies  he had touched

Amplexus      ille  utrumque  et  carpens  oscula,
(having) embraced  He  each of them  and  picking   kisses
                               getting

dulcemque    in    ambos  caritatem   partiens,
and the sweet  towards  both   love   apportioning

"Cotidie" inquit "speculo vos  uti  volo.  Tu   ne
Every day  he said  the mirror  you  to use  I want  You (son)  lest

formam      corrumpas    nequitiae     malis.
(your) beauty  you corrupt  of wickedness  by bad deeds

Tu faciem ut istam moribus
You (daughter) countenance in order that that by habits

vincas bonis."
you overcome good

# IX. Socrates ad Amicos

----

## IX. Socrates ad Amicos
Socrates to (his) Friends

**Vulgare amici nomen sed rara est fides.**
Common (is) of "friend" the name but rare is faithfulness

**Cum parvas aedes sibi fundasset Socrates**
When a small house for himself had built Socrates
{aedispl}

**(cuius mortem non fugio si famam adsequar, et**
(whose death not I flee if (such) fame I achieve and
avoid

**cedo invidiae dummodo absolvar cinis),**
I yield to envy if only I will be acquitted (when) ash
after my death)

**ex populo sic nescioquis, ut fieri**
from the common people thus I don't know who as to happen

**solet:**
is customary

"Quaeso,     talis     vir    tam   angustam   ponis
I ask     (you) so great   a man   so     narrow     you erect

domum?"
a house

"Utinam" inquit "veris    hanc    amicis impleam!"
Would that   he said   with true   this (house)   friends    I may fill

# X. Poeta de Credere et non Credere

----

X. Poeta   de   Credere   et   non   Credere
A Poet  about  Believe  and  not  Believe

Periculosum  est  credere     et     non  credere.
Dangerous   it is  to believe  as well as  not  to believe

Utriusque   rei   exemplum  breviter  adponam.
Of both   things   an example   shortly   I will adduce

Hippolytus  obiit,   quia     novercae     creditum est;
Hippolytus   died   because  (his) stepmother   believed   is
                                                 people believed

Cassandrae  quia  non  creditum,     ruit     Ilium.
for Cassandra  because  not  (was) belief  went under  Troy

Ergo       exploranda   est  veritas  multum,  prius
Therefore  to be investigated  is  the truth  much  before

quam  stulte  prava     iudicet     sententia.
()   foolishly  a crooked  gives judgment   opinion

Sed, ne fabulosam vetustatem elevem, narrabo
However, lest a mythical antiquity I raise I will narrate

tibi quod factum est mea memoria.
to you what happened is (within) my memory
has

Maritus erat qui diligebat coniugem. Togam
a husband there was who loved (his) wife a toga

puram iam paravit filio. Seductus in
white already he provided for (his) son (He was) taken aside in

secretum a liberto suo est, sperante heredem
secret by freedman his own is hoping (as) heir
was

suffici se proximum.
to be substituted himself (the) next
the son being disinherited, he would become heir

Libertus iste de puero multa mentitus
Freedman that about the boy many things said lying

est et plura de flagitiis castae
he was/had and still more about shameful acts chaste

mulieris adiecit: id quod sentiebat maxime
of (his) wife he added (namely) that what he felt most
{pf}

doliturum · amanti: · ventitare · adulterum
would sting · a loving man · to come often · an adulterer
· · that came often

stuproque · turpi · pollui · famam
and (that) by a defilement · shameful · to be · the good name
· · was dishonored

domus.
of the house

Incensus · ille · falso · crimine · uxoris
Incensed · he · by the pretended · crime · of (his) wife

simulavit · iter · ad · villam, · clamque · in
he simulated · a trip · to · (his) country house · and secretly · in

oppido · subsedit. · Deinde · noctu · subito · ianuam
town · remained · Thereupon · at night · suddenly · the door

intravit, · recta · cubiculum · uxoris · petens, · in
he entered · straight · bedroom · of (his) wife · making for · in

quo · dormire · mater · natum · iusserat, · aetatem
which · to sleep · the mother · (her) son · had ordered · (his) age

adultam · servans · diligentius.
adult · guarding · (even) more assiduously

| Dum | quaerunt | lumen, | dum | concursant |
|---|---|---|---|---|
| While | people seek | a light | while | run about |

| familia, | irae | furentis | impetum |
|---|---|---|---|
| the (members of) the household | of the wrath | raging | the fury |

| non | sustinens | ad | lectum | vadit, | temptat | in |
|---|---|---|---|---|---|---|
| not | restraining | to | the bed | he goes | feels for | in |

| tenebris | caput. |
|---|---|
| the darkness | a head |

| Ut | sentit | tonsum, | gladio | pectus |
|---|---|---|---|---|
| As soon as | he feels | (a) shaven (head) | with a sword | the chest |

| transigit, | nihil | respiciens | dum | dolorem |
|---|---|---|---|---|
| he transfixes | nothing | caring for | as long as | t(his) grief |

| vindicet. |
|---|
| he may avenge |

| Lucerna | adlata, | simul | adspexit |
|---|---|---|---|
| A lamp | having been brought up | simultaneously | he looks at |

| filium | sanctamque | uxorem | dormientem | illum |
|---|---|---|---|---|
| the son | and (his) sacred pure | wife | sleeping | (to) him |

**prope, sopita  primo  somno  quae  nil  senserat.**
close  asleep  (in) the first  sleep  who  nothing  had noticed

**Repraesentavit  in  se  poenam  facinoris**
He executes  towards  himself  the penalty  of (his) misdeed

**et  ferro  incubuit  quod  credulitas**
and  upon the iron sword  he lay down / threw himself  which (sword)  credulity

**strinxerat.**
had drawn
made him draw

**Accusatores  postularunt  mulierem,  Romamque**
(The) prosecutors  summoned  the woman  and to Rome

**pertraxerunt  ad  centumviros.**
dragged (her)  to  (the) commissioned judges

**Maligna  suspicio  insontem  deprimit,**
A malign  suspicion (woman)  the guiltless (woman)  weighed upon

**quod  bona  possideat.  Stant**
because  the goods estate  she had come into possession of  Stand firm

**patroni  fortiter  causam  tuentes  innocentis**
her patrons advocates  strongly  the cause  defending  of the innocent

feminae.
woman

A divo Augusto tum petierunt iudices ut
From the divine Augustus then asked the judges that

adiuvaret iuris iurandi fidem,
he would assist (them) of the law to swear the faithful discharge

quod ipsos implicuisset error criminis.
because them thad entangled the error of the crime
embarrassed intricacy

Qui, postquam tenebras calumniae
Who (Augustus) after the darkness of the false accusation

dispulit certumque fontem veritatis repperit,
he had dispelled and the certain source of truth had found

"Luat" inquit "poenas libertus causa
Let undergo he said the penalties the freedman (who is) the cause

mali; namque orbam nato simul
of (this) evil and because (she is) bereft of a son at the same time

et privatam viro, miserandam potius quam
and derived of (her) man (that) to be pitied rather than

damnandam existimo.
to be condemned I estimate (she is)

Quod si delata crimina paterfamilias
Because if the reported crimes the father of the family

perscrutatus esset, si mendacium subtiliter
scrutinized were if the falsehood exactly
had

limasset, a radicibus, non evertisset
he had investigated by the roots not he would have overturned

scelere funesto domum."
by a crime calamitous the house

Nil spernat auris, nec tamen
Nothing let he wave aside from the ears neither however

credat statim, quandoquidem et illi peccant
let he believe at once because too those sin

quos minime putes, et qui non peccant
whom the least you guess and who not do sin

impugnantur fraudibus.
are assailed with deceitful (accusations)

Hoc admonere simplices etiam potest, ne
This warn the simple (minds) also can that not
                                                may

opinione alterius quid ponderent.
on the opinion of somebody else something they may judge
                                              {pondero}

Ambitio namque dissidens mortalium aut
The ambition For diverse of mortal men either

gratiae subscribit aut odio suo.
to (its) favour assents or to hatred its

Erit ille notus quem per te
will be He well-known whom by your(self)

cognoveris.
you will have known

Haec exsecutus sum propterea
These (events) described I am for this reason
                                      have

pluribus, brevitate nimia quoniam quosdam
with more (details) brevity too great because some persons

offendimus.
we have offended

# XI. Eunuchus ad Improbum

----

XI. Eunuchus ad Improbum
The eunuch    to        a Knave

Eunuchus    litigabat    cum    quodam    improbo,    qui
An eunuch    had a quarrel    with    some    knave    who

super    obscena    dicta    et    petulans    iurgium
on top of    obscene    sayings    and    petulant    contention

damnum    insectatus    est    amissi    corporis.
the loss    upbraided    is    of the lost    body (part)
                          has    missing

"En"    ait    "hoc    est    unum    cur
Look    said (the eunuch)    this    is    the one (thing)    why

laborem    validius,    integritatis    testes
I exert myself    more strongly    of (my) integrity    witnesses(=testicles)

quia    desunt    mihi.    Sed    quid    Fortunae,    stulte,
because    are lacking    to me    But    what    of Fortune    you fool

delictum   arguis?   Id   demum   est   homini   turpe
the fault   you blame   That   finally   is   to a man   scandalous

quod   meruit   pati."
what   he has deserved   to suffer

# XII. Pullus ad Margaritam

----

XII.    Pullus    ad  Margaritam
The Chicken   to    the Pearl

In  sterculino  pullus  gallinacius  dum   quaerit  escam
In    a dunghill   a pullet    chicken    while  it looks for    food

margaritam  repperit.
  a pearl        finds
           {pf}

"Quanta       res      indigno    loco  iaces!"  inquit
(You) how (fine)  a thing  in an unworthy  place  you lay  he says
                                lies

Hoc  si   quis    pretii  tui  cupidus    vidisset,
This   If  somebody  of value  your  desirous   would have seen

    olim             redisses        ad   splendorem
    once      you would have returned   to    splendor
already for some time

pristinum.
(your) former

Quod ego te inveri, cui potior multo
That I you have found for whom more preferable much

est cibus, nec tibi prodesse nec mihi
is food neither for you be useful nor for me

quicquam potest."
anything can

Hoc illis narro qui me non intellegunt.
This to those I tell who me (do) not understand

# XIII. Apes et Fuci Vespa Iudice

----

XIII.  Apes   et   Fuci      Vespa      Iudice
The Bees  and  the Drones  (with) the Wasp  (as) Judge

Apes    in  alta  quercu  fecerant  favos.
The bees  in  a high    oak      had made    hives

Hos            fuci      inertes  esse  dicebant  suos.
Those (hives)  the drones  inactive  to be    said      theirs

Lis       ad  forum  deducta  est,    vespa       iudice;
The dispute  to    court    brought    is    (with) the wasp  (as) judge

quae,  genus  utrumque   cum      nosset  pulcherrime,
which  kind(s)      both    because  he knew      very well

legem   duabus  hanc  proposuit  partibus:
law    to the two  this    proposed      parties
rule

"Non  inconveniens  corpus  et  par  est  color,   ut
Not        dissimilar      the body  and  alike  is    the color  so that

**plane in dubium res merito venerit.**
clearly into doubt the matter deservedly has come

**Sed, ne religio mea peccet imprudens,**
However lest scrupulousness my sin unawares
                                          may err

**alvos accipite et opus infundite ceris,**
hives take and (your) work pour into the wax(en cells)

**ut ex sapore mellis et forma**
in order that from flavor of the honey and the shape

**favi,**
of the hive

**de quis nunc agitur, auctor horum**
about which now is the matter the maker of those

**appareat."**
may become clear

**Fuci recusant, apibus conditio placet.**
The drones refuse to the bees the condition pleases

**Tunc illa talem rettulit sententiam: "Apertum**
Then she such pronounces a sentence Uncovered
     the wasp

est quis non possit et quis fecerit. Quapropter
is who not is able and who made (it) Therefore

apibus fructum restituo suum."
to the bees fruit I restitute their own
product

Hanc praeterissem fabulam silentio, si
this I would have passed over fable in silence if

pactam fuci non recusassent fidem.
(their) pledged the drones not would not have refused faith
promise

# XIV. De Lusu et Seueritate

----

XIV. De     Lusu    et Severitate
About (the) Play and    Severity
                        (Seriousness)

Puerorum   in   turba   quidam   ludentem   Atticus
Boys       in   crowd   some     played     from Attica
                                            (Athens)

Aesopum      nucibus      cum vidisset,      restitit,
Aesop     (with playing) nuts when  (he) saw   set himself against
                                            (played along)

et  quasi  delirum  risit.  Quod  sensit     simul
and like   crazy    laughed But   (he) felt  simultaneously

derisor  potius  quam  deridendus   senex,    arcum
derision (of) power as    laughed   (an) old man (a) bow

retensum posuit in   media    via:
unstrung (he) set in (the) middle (of the) road

"Heus" inquit "sapiens, expedi quid fecerim."
Hey     asked    wise    explain what (I) have done

Concurrit populus. Ille se torquet diu, nec
Throng (the) people He himself throws long nor

quaestionis positae causam intellegit.
question levies case understands

Novissime succumbit. Tum victor sophus:
(At) last succumbs Then (the) victor (is) wisdom

"Cito rumpes arcum, semper se tensum
Quickly (you will) break (the) bow always if stretched

habueris; at si laxaris, cum voles erit utilis."
you had but if (you) relax (it) when (you) want (it) is useful

Sic lusus animo debent aliquando dari, ad
Thus play (the) mind must sometimes to give to

cogitandum melior ut redeat tibi.
think better as return (to) you

# XV. Canis ad Agnum

----

XV.  Canis  ad  Agnum
The Dog  to  the Lamb

Inter     capellas      agno      palanti     canis      "Stulte"
Among    the goats    to the lamb   bleating   the dog:    You fool

inquit "erras; non est hic mater tua."
he says  you err   not   is   here  mother  your

Ovesque      segregatas  ostendit  procul.
And the sheep  by themselves  he points to  at a distance

"Non     illam      quaero      quae     cum     libitum est
Not       her      do I look for    who     when    pleasing  it is
                                                     pleases her

concipit,  dein  portat    onus     ignotum     certis
conceives (me)  then  carries  the burden  unknown    certain
                                                      (a number of)

mensibus,        novissime      prolapsam      effundit
during months      newest        slipped out     brought forth
                  (in the end)

sarcinam;   verum   illam   quae   me   nutrit
the load   but   her   who   me   nourishes

admoto   ubere,   fraudatque   natos
moved towards (me)   with (her) udder   and defrauds   her childeren

lacte   ne   desit mihi."
of milk   so that not   it lacks   to me

"Tamen   illa   est potior quae   te   peperit."
Yet   that one   it is   rather   who   to you   gave birth

"Non   ita.   Beneficium   sane   magnum   natali
Not   so   benefit   indeed   a great   by (my) birth

dedit,   ut   expectarem   lanium   in
she has given   in order that   I would expect   the butcher   within

horas   singulas!
hours   a few

Unde   illa   scivit   niger   an   albus   nascerer?
Whereby   she   has known   black   or   white   I would be born

Age   porro,   parere   si   voluisset   feminam,
Well   then   to give birth to   if   she had wanted   a female

quid     profecisset     cum   crearer   masculus?
what   profit would it have given  when  I was created     male

Cuius    potestas nulla in gignendo  fuit,    cur
She whose   power     no   in  giving birth  has been  wherefore
         (control)

   sit     potior  hac  quae     iacentis
she would be  preferable  to her  who  of the (lamb) laying down

  miserita    est,  dulcemque   sponte   praestat
had compassion   has   and sweet  spontaneously  'provides

benevolentiam?
benevolence

Facit  parentes  bonitas,  non  necessitas."
makes   parents  Goodness  not   necessity

His     versibus   demonstrare  voluit    auctor
By these    verses     to show    wanted  the author
                             {pf}

obsistere  homines  legibus,  meritis  capi.
oppose  (that) people  laws  but by merits  are won

# XVI. Cicada et Noctua

----

**XVI. Cicada et Noctua**
The Grasshopper and the Night Owl

**Humanitati qui se non accommodat**
humaneness (he) who himself not accomodates

**plerumque poenas oppetit superbiae.**
often the punishment meets of his arrogance

**Cicada acerbum convicium faciebat**
A grasshopper shrill noise was making
(bothersome)

**noctuae, solitae victum in tenebris**
to the night owl (which) is used to food in the darkness

**quaerere, cavoque ramo capere somnum**
to search for and (in) a hollow tree branch take sleep

**interdiu.**
on the day

Rogata est ut taceret. Multo validius clamare
asked She is that she be silent much stronger to scream
was

occepit. Rursus admonita, prece accensa
she began Again admonished, by the request kindled
{pf}

magis est. Noctua, ut vidit sibi nullum
more she is The night owl as she saw for herself nothing
was {pf} no

esse auxilium et verba contemni sua, hac
to be help and (her) words to go unheeded her with this

fallacia est adgressa garrulam:
stratagem is approached the loquacious
(has)

"Dormire quia me non sinunt cantus tui, sonare
sleep As me not let songs your to sound

citharam quos putes Apollinis, potare
(like) the cither which you think of Apollo to drink

est animus nectar, quod Pallas mihi nuper
there is a mind nectar which Pallas Athene to me recently
I would like

donavit; si non fastidis, veni; una bibamus."
has given if not you dislike (it) come together let us drink
{abl}

| Illa, | quae | arebat | siti, | simul | gaudebat |
|-------|------|--------|-------|-------|----------|
| She | who | was parched | by thirst | at the same time | was happy |

| vocem | suam | laudari, | cupide | advolavit. |
|-------|------|----------|--------|------------|
| (her) voice | her | to be praised | eagerly | flew near |

| Noctua, | obsepto | cavo, | trepidantem |
|---------|---------|-------|-------------|
| The night owl | having closed | from the cavity | the flapping about |

| consectata | est | et | leto | dedit. |
|------------|-----|-----|------|--------|
| followed (it) | is has | and | to death | gave (it) {pf} |

| Sic, | quod | negabat | viva, | tribuit | mortua. |
|------|------|---------|-------|---------|---------|
| Thus | (that) what | she denied | being alive | she granted | being dead {pf} |

# XVII. Arbores in Deorum Tutela

----

XVII.  Arbores  in  Deorum  Tutela
The Trees  in  of the Gods  the Protection
under

Olim  divi  legerunt  arbores  quas  esse  in  sua
Once  the gods  chose  the trees  which  to be  in  their
under

tutela  vellent.  Quercus  Iovi,  at  myrtus
protection  they wanted  The oak  to Jupiter  and  the myrtle

Veneri  placuit,  Phoebo  laurea,  pinus
to Venus  pleased  to Apollo  the laurel tree  the pine tree
{pf}

Cybelae,  populus  celsa  Herculi.
to Cybele  the poplar  tall  to Hercules

Minerva  admirans  quare  steriles  sumerent
Minerva  wondering  why  inproductive (trees)  they took

interrogavit.  Causam  dixit  Iuppiter:
inquired  The cause  said  Jupiter
{pf}          told

"Honorem fructu ne videamur
(our) honor for the fruit In order that not we would seem
dignity

vendere."
to sell

"Statim dixit Minerva "At mehercules nobis vero
At once said Minerva But by Hercules to us indeed
{pf}

oliva propter fructum est gratior."
the olive tree because of (its) fruit is more dear

Tum sic deorum genitor atque hominum
Then so (said) of the gods the father and of men

sator:
the sower
creator

"O nata, merito sapiens diceris omnibus. Nisi
Oh daughter justly wise you are said by all If not

utile est quod facimus, stulta est gloria."
useful is (that) what we make foolish is glory
do

Nihil agere quod non prosit fabella admonet.
nothing to do which not is useful The fable admonishes (us)

# XVIII. Pauo ad Iunonem de uoce sua

----

XVIII.    Pavo    ad Iunonem   de  voce sua
       The Peacock  to    Juno    about voice his

Pavo    ad Iunonem   venit,   indigne ferens quod
A Peacock  to    Juno    came/{pf} indignantly bearing tat
                     indignant

cantus    luscinii    sibi   non   tribuerit;
the singing of the nightingale to himself not she had assigned

illum    esse   cunctis  auribus  mirabilem,
(that) it  to be  for all   ears   wonderful
the nightingale was

se    derideri   simul  ac  vocem
(but) he himself to be laughed at at the same time and (her) voice
                 as soon as

miserit.
he sent
let out

Tunc  consolandi   gratia  dixit dea:
Then of comforting (him) fot the sake said the goddess
    in order to comfort (her)  {pf}

"Sed forma vincis, vincis magnitudine; nitor
But in shape you win you win as for size the splendor
{abl}

smaragdi collo praefulget tuo, pictisque plumis
of the emerald neck shines forth on your with colored feathers

gemmeam caudam explicas."
jeweled a tail you unfold

"Quo mi" inquit "mutam speciem si vincor
Why for me she said mute beauty if I am defeated

sono?"
as for the sound

"Fatorum arbitrio partes sunt vobis datae; tibi
of fate by the decision the parts are to you granted to you
{pl}

forma, vires aquilae, luscinio melos,
the shape the strength to the eagle to the nightingale the melody
beauty {pl}

augurium corvo, laeva cornici omina;
the prediction to the raven unfavorable to the crow omens

omnesque propriis sunt contentae dotibus.
and all with their own are content endowments

**Noli       adfectare    quod    tibi  non  est  datum,**
Do not want    aspire to    (that) what  to you  not  is  given

**delusa   ne   spes ad querelam reccidat."**
deluded  that not  hope  to  a complaint  reverts to

# XIX. Aesopus Respondet Garrulo

----

XIX.   Aesopus   Respondet   Garrulo
19       Aesop        answers     to-the-garrulous

Cum   Aesopus   esset   solus   domino     familia,        est
When     Aesop        was    the-only    chief    for-the-family  (he) is

iussus     parare   cenam   maturius.
ordered  to-prepare   dinner      earlier

Ergo          quaerens     ignem     lustravit       aliquot
Therefore       seeking        fire     he-traversed   to-some-other

domus,     tandemque     invenit     ubi     accenderet
house         and-finally       finds     where     he-fired-up

lucernam.   Tum     quod       fuerat       circumeunti
the-lantern    Then    because   he-had-been      going-around

longius     iter     effecit     brevius:     namque     coepit
the-longer    trip    he-made     shorter        for         he-began

redire   recta   per   forum.
to-return   right   through   the-market

Et   quidam   garrulus   e   turba:
And   some   talkative   from   the-crowd

"Aesope,   quid   cum   lumine   medio   sole?"
Aesop   why   with   a-light   in-the-middle   (of) the-sun
(do you have)   (of day)

"Hominem"   inquit   "quaero."   Et   abiit
A-man   he-responds   I-look-for   And   goes-away

festinans   domum.
rushing   to-the-house

Hoc   si   molestus   ille   ad   animum   rettulit,
This   if   tiresome-man   that   to   his-mind   had-brought-back

sensit   profecto   se   hominem   non   uisum
he-feels   actually   himself   (as a) man   not   viewed

seni,   intempestiue   qui   occupato
by-the-old (Aesop)   unseasonably   who   with-the-busy (one)
(always)

adluserit.
plays
(makes jokes)